Introduction

This book provides a framework ~~~~~~~~~~~~~~~~~~~~ to allow students
to examine one aspect of the role that science and technology play
in modern society, namely, how they are involved in industrial
development and war. By doing this it is hoped that the participants
(students and teachers) will be better equipped to make up their
own minds on what a desirable pattern of scientific research and
development might be, on what are the problems of organizing them
and managing them, and on how they relate to political and
economic structures.

Our approach will be to identify problem areas, to ask questions
and to point to the relevant sources that will enable you to begin to
answer these questions. This approach is predicated by the view that
there are no 'right' answers and that in most of the problem areas we
identify there are, and should be, disagreements. In summary, the
central questions this book will pose, and hopes to help answer, are:

(i) How did it come about that science and technology absorb such
large resources in modern industrial society?

(ii) In what ways are scientific and technological developments shaped
by economic, political and social factors? Are the contemporary
problems with regard to science and technology problems of
science and technology *per se,* or problems of our social systems?

(iii) What have been and are the relationships between science and
technology? How has industrialization altered the nature and
development of science?

(iv) What have been the important features of the scientization of
war?

Each chapter consists of: (1) a *Text* which introduces the topic
and identifies problems. This Text is based upon and itself introduces: (2) *Essential and Related Reading.* The books and articles
listed as essential reading are an integral part of the text and *must*
be read to fully cover the topic. Both the Essential Reading and
Bibliography are keyed to: (3) *Questions and Points for Discussion or
Essay Topics,* which it is hoped will help to focus students' work on
each chapter.

We would like to thank various colleagues, too numerous to
mention, who have commented on earlier versions of the material
in this book. We would also like to thank Dr. W.F. Williams for his
assistance and encouragement in all stages of the production of the
book.

Chapter One
Technology and Science in the
Industrial Revolution

The question we want to discuss in this first chapter is: what part did technology and science play in the Industrial Revolution in Britain? There are a number of reasons for beginning with this topic. Firstly, it provides an excellent case study for looking at the relationships between science, technology and industrial development. Secondly, it provides an opportunity to learn something about the development of the first industrial nation — Britain. Consideration of this topic may also throw light on an interesting connection, which many have supposed, but which has been difficult to substantiate, between the Scientific and Industrial Revolutions. This matter also relates to a continuing controversy amongst certain historians about the exact role of science in the Industrial Revolution in Britain. Many of these issues have implications beyond those of the interpretation of a single historical event. For example, with regard to developing countries, there is considerable debate about whether the establishment of scientific institutions and the 'organization' of technical innovation are necessary prerequisites of industrialization and modernization. It may be that there are lessons to be learnt from the experience of early industrialization of today's developed nations.

The Industrial Revolution in Britain

What then was the Industrial Revolution? In the view of the leading economic historian Eric Hobsbawm, it was 'the most fundamental transformation of human life in the history of the world recorded in written documents.' According to David Landes 'it was the Industrial Revolution that initiated a cumulative, self-sustaining advance in technology whose repercussions would be felt in all aspects of economic life.' Again, Landes tells us that: 'the heart of the Industrial Revolution was an interrelated succession of technological changes combined with new forms of industrial organization.' The main technological changes were: (1) the substitution of mechanical devices for human labor and skill; (2) the replacement of animal and human strength by inanimate power; (3) the improved getting and working of raw materials. The main organizational changes were associated with the factory system of production — its discipline, division of labor, employer—worker relationship and increase in the size of productive units.

Important as these factors were, the Industrial Revolution was something more than this: it was also a major social and political transformation. It created new classes and new class relationships in society. The British ruling class were little affected to begin with, except that they became richer, but eventually a new class, the industrial bourgoisie, took greater economic and political power. In opposition to this new ruling class emerged another new grouping: the proletariat or industrial working class. Associated with the rise of the industrial bourgoisie came what has been termed 'economism', or the imposition of the 'cash nexus' on all aspects of life. Selling one's labor for a cash wage became the only possible source of income for the great mass of people. The major social changes were urbanization and 'modernization'. The industrial working class became concentrated in big cities: in 1750 there were only two cities in Britain with more than 50 000 inhabitants; by 1851 there were 29 and in the same year, for the first time, more people lived in towns than in the country. Modernization is usually taken to include the following: greater regularity and routine; greater social mobility and mixing; the displacement of 'old' traditions, wisdom and morality; and the greater diffusion of 'rational attitudes' and knowledge.

The Industrial Revolution is a complex subject and all we have done is to review a number of its more important features. We have not gone into its origins and causes, nor discussed its human results, nor mentioned its international dimension. One problem in discussing a topic like the Industrial Revolution is that one is dealing with 'the most complex kind of problem, one that involves numerous factors of variable weight working in changing combinations.' However, this is not to say the matter is impossible to discuss; rather it is to underline the need to specify carefully those aspects of the subject one wishes to investigate. From our interest in the relationships between science, technology and industrial development we can specify two questions:

1. How was technical change related to economic change in this period?
2. How was technical change related to science and to developments in scientific theory and practice?

The first question is essentially one for economic historians to answer and according to Hobsbawm, given that the Industrial Revolution was a product of a capitalist society, 'the puzzle lies in the relationship between making a profit and technological change.' Various studies have suggested the general conclusion that technical change responded primarily to economic stimuli and conditions. In other words, technical change and innovation were 'economic activities'. We would like to illustrate these general points by reference to the cotton textile industry, unquestionably the key sector in early British industrialization.

Technical change and the Industrial Revolution

Before the Industrial Revolution, Britain, like much of the rest of Europe, was not underdeveloped or undeveloped like developing countries in the twentieth century. It had a buoyant economic system, supported by government policy, which was probably a necessary precondition for industrialization. The crucial changes in the industrialization of Britain were the shift of resources from agriculture to manufacturing and from a commercial system centered on trade to an industrial one centered on production.

Trade in manufactures, of which textiles were an important part, grew steadily from the late Middle Ages, but took on a new significance with the rise of mercantile capitalism. Trade was controlled by merchants, who were 'middle men' between manufacturers and their raw materials and markets, and often between town and country. The merchants lived and profited by trade. They sought expanded markets, particularly overseas markets where monopolies brought high profits. The essential point is that the main concern of the merchants were the terms of trade, markets and transport.

In the century or so before 1780 a number of factors in this situation changed. Trading in overseas markets became more secure through improvements in transportation and the security provided by powerful naval fleets. In the case of Britain the government pursued an aggressive foreign policy in support of lucrative overseas trade. However, the changing circumstances intensified competition and led some states to institute protectionist policies. In Britain these changes were accompanied by a growth in the demand for manufactures in the domestic market owing to the effects of the rising standard of living and population growth. One result of these changes was that merchants and traders became concerned about demand not being met and over time came to interest themselves much more centrally with production. In the case of cotton textiles there were pressures to increase production and to cut production costs.

Responsibility for the production of cotton textiles had rested with master weavers who contracted out work to spinners and weavers working in their own homes. This work had moved increasingly to the rural areas to take advantage of lower costs. The further pressures on master weavers to reduce costs led them gradually, but unevenly, to reduce contracting out and replace it by 'collective producing organizations' or factories. The use of factories facilitated the control of working hours and wages, it enabled more intensive use of tools and machines and it allowed for specialization and the division of labor. These moves were so successful that they may well have retarded mechanization in this sector to some extent. Nonetheless, it is clear that a combination of economic forces and organizational conditions made cotton textiles ripe for mechanization. The story of mechanization of cotton textiles in the late eighteenth century is well known; the spinning jenny, the water-frame and the mule first revolutionized cotton spinning, whilst later the flying-shuttle and power loom radically altered weaving. It is perhaps worth emphasizing that there were time-lags between the invention of these devices and their adoption and widespread use. The essential point remains that cotton textile factories offered opportunities for mechanization, the use of power and the exploitation of new technologies. Such improvements in production required significant capital investment, but they offered good returns.

Science and the Industrial Revolution

The example of cotton textiles shows that technical change largely responded to economic needs and, at least by implication, it suggests that technical change was not critically dependent upon developments in science. Certainly none of the inventions in the mechanization of cotton textiles appears to be in any way directly dependent on new scientific knowledge or the activities of men of science. Hobsbawm offers some views on this:

> The early Industrial Revolution was technically rather primitive, not because no better science and technology was available or because men took no interest in it or could not be persuaded to use it. It was simply because, by and large, the application of simple ideas available for centuries, often by no means expensive, could produce startling results.

It is usually argued that there was little or no interaction between science and technical change in the Industrial Revolution in most industries. For example, the iron (and steel) industry is said to have learnt nothing from chemistry (N.B. metallurgy did not exist) until the last quarter of the nineteenth century. The only exception usually allowed is the chemical industry, where new techniques in bleaching seem to have depended on new chemical understanding. The development of the steam engine is more controversial, but it is often said that here science learnt from technology. However, none of these cases are open and shut, so the further study of any would prove illuminating of the relationships between science and technology.

In a review of the debate on the role of science in the Industrial Revolution, Peter Mathias, in line with the majority view, concluded that 'in the immediate context of manufacture, formal scientific knowledge was much less strategic in determining commercial success than some modern studies have suggested.' The modern studies to which he refers are principally those of Musson and Robinson, who, through detailed studies of late eighteenth century scientific societies, have shown that there was considerable social interaction between manufacturers and men of science and that many manufacturers were 'scientifically minded'. While not denying this, Mathias points to the lack of evidence that the joint activities of manufacturers and men of science produced any invention or innovation of strategic economic importance.

Yet, there is no denying that during the Industrial Revolution there was considerable interest in science, a growing number of scientific societies and that these were often associated with technical ambition. If we accept that scientific knowledge and the activities of manufacturers and men of science contributed little or nothing to technical change, how do we account for the currency of science in this period? At least two answers can be offered. Firstly, Mathias suggests that 'scientific attitudes were much more widespread and diffused than scientific knowledge'. What scientific attitudes might have been has been elaborated by Landes:

> Rationality and what we may call the Faustian sense of mastery over man and nature . . . . Science indeed was the perfect bridge between rationality and mastery; it was the application of reason to the understanding of natural and, with time, human phenomena; and it made possible a more effective response to, or manipulation of, the natural and human environment.

It is interesting that in a different context Hobsbawm refers to the rigorous rationality that was applied to methods of production and organization. Secondly, more recent work on late eighteenth century scientific societies has suggested that 'science served a very important function in the cultural legitimation of modern urban and industrial society'. Science seemed to embody the progressive, anti-authoritarian and down-to-earth attitudes of the new men of industrial Britain; it was also practical and commonsensical. Yet, science was still 'polite knowledge'; it was respectable, ordered and theologically approved. In this context, Shapin suggests that 'the *utility* of science has to be pried loose from its purely economic associations and must be seen as a far more diffuse and vital concept'. Again, these two explanations deserve further enquiry, especially as they offer new insights into issues raised previously.

Reading

ESSENTIAL

1. Mathias, P. (1972). 'Who Unbound Prometheus? Science and technical change 1600–1800.' In *Science and Society 1600–1900.*

Ed. P. Mathias. Cambridge, Cambridge University Press
A review of the 'debate' on the role of science in the Industrial
Revolution.
2. Furtado, C. (1964). *Development and Underdevelopment*, 96–109.
Chicago, Chicago University Press
Very readable account of the origins of technical change in
European industrialization.
3. Thackray, A. (1974). 'The Industrial Revolution and the Image of
Science.' In *Science and Values*. Ed. A. Thackray and E.
Mendelsohn. New York, Humanities Press
Useful introductory discussion of the cultural role of science.

RELATED

The Industrial Revolution
4. Deane, P. (1965). *The First Industrial Nation.* Cambridge,
Cambridge University Press
A standard economic history textbook, useful chapters on individual industries, but ignores science
5. Hobsbawm, E.J. (1968). *Industry and Empire.* London, Weidenfeld
and Nicolson
See Chapters 2–4. Readable and stimulating; probably the best
modern account
6. Landes, D.S. (1969). *The Unbound Prometheus.* Cambridge,
Cambridge University Press
See Introduction and Chapter 2. Originally written as a history of
technological development, so unsurprising that most historians
feel it gives too much attention to technology!
7. Mantoux, P. (1928). *The Industrial Revolution in the Eighteenth
Century.* New York, University Paperbacks (1964)
After 50 years remains a standard work.

The Scientific and Industrial Revolutions
8. Bernal, J.D. (1954). *Science in History.* New York, Watts; London,
Penguin (1969)
Encyclopaedic, but a useful introduction
9. Easlea, B. (1974). *Liberation and the Aims of Science.* London,
Chatto and Windus
See Chapter 4 'Political Commitments in the Age of the
Scientific and Industrial Revolutions'
10. Kearney, H. (1971). *Science and Change 1500–1700.* World
University Library
See Chapter 8. Readable, original and with lots of good
illustrations.
11. Mathias, P. (1970). 'The Scientific and Industrial Revolutions'.
Minerva, **10,** No. 2

A review of Musson and Robinson but raises the wider question
of links between the two Revolutions

Relationships between science and technology

12. Cardwell, D.S.L. (1972). *Technology, Science and History*.
London, Heinemann
See Chapters 3 and 4. Essentially history of technology, but links
with science and the economy are not ignored.
13. Gillispie, C.C. (1957). 'The Natural History of Industry'. *Isis*, **48**,
398–407
Shows how French scientific supremacy was not in itself a
sufficient condition for industrialization
14. Hall, R.A. (1974). 'What Did the Industrial Revolution in
Britain Owe to Science?' In *Historical Perspectives Studies in
English Thought and Society in Honour of J.H. Plumb*, 129–151.
Ed. N. McKendrick. London, Europa
Argues the negative case
15. Lilley, S. (1970). 'Technological Progress and the Industrial
Revolution.' In *Economic History of Europe, Volume 3*. Ed.
C.M. Cipolla. London, Fontana
Quite a good introduction, but technological determinist
16. Mathias, P. (1975). 'Skills and the diffusion of innovations from
Britain in the 18th century.' *Transactions of the Royal Historical
Society*, **25**, 93–113
A good discussion of the sources of technical change
17. Musson, A.E. (Ed.) (1972). *Science, Technology and Economic
Growth in the Eighteenth Century*. New York, University Paperbacks
This book has an excellent introduction and is a good collection
of essays; includes references 1, 13 and 21

Social history of science

18. McKendrick, N. (1973). 'The Role of Science in the Industrial
Revolution: A study of Josiah Wedgwood as a scientist and
industrial chemist.' In *Changing Perspectives in the History of
Science: Essays in Honour of Joseph Needham*, 274–319. Ed. M.
Teich and R.M. Young. London, Heinemann
A stimulating biographical treatment of the question
19. Musson, A.E. and Robinson, E. (1969). *Science and Technology
in the Industrial Revolution*. Manchester, Manchester UP
Meticulously researched series of studies showing close links
between men of science and men of industry
20. Porter, R. (1973). 'The Industrial Revolution and the Rise of the
Science of Geology.' In Ref. 18, pp. 320–343
Shows that the popular science of geology contributed little or
nothing to mining.
21. Schofield, R.E. (1963). *The Lunar Society of Birmingham. A*

social history of provincial science and industry in 18th century England. Oxford, Oxford University Press

A detailed study of this famous society; see pp. 436—440 for summary of the main argument. A short article on 'The industrial orientation of science in the Lunar Society', by the same author, will be found in *Isis,* **48**, 408—416 (1957)

22. Shapin, S. (1972). 'The Pottery Philosophical Society 1819—1835 — an Examination of the Cultural Uses of Provincial Science.' *Science Studies,* **2**, 311—336

    Discusses a later period than many of the other studies, but an introduction to a new perspective
23. Thackray, A. (1974). 'Natural Knowledge in Cultural Context: the Manchester Model.' *American Historical Review,* **LXXIX**, 672—709

    A very stimulating study of the Manchester Lit. and Phil.
24. Thackray, A. (1970). 'Science, Technology and the Industrial Revolution.' *History of Science,* **9**, 76—89

    A brief reappraisal of the life and work of John Dalton

ADDENDUM: SPECIFIC INDUSTRIES

Textiles
Cardwell, D.S.L. Ref. 12, pp. 75—79 and 94—101
Deane, P. Ref. 4, Chapter 6
Mantoux, P. Ref. 7, Part II, Chapter 2

Steam power
Cardwell, D.S.L. 'Science and the Steam Engine 1790—1825.' In Ref. 1
Kerker, M. (1961). 'Science and the Steam Engine.' *Technology and Culture,* **2**, No. 4
Mantoux, P. Ref. 7, Part I, Chapter 4

Chemicals
Clow, A. and Clow, N. (1952). *The Chemical Revolution: a contribution to social history.* New York, Books for Libraries
Haber, L.F. (1958). *The Chemical Industry in the Nineteenth Century.* Oxford, Oxford University Press

Machines
Deane, P. Ref. 4, Chapter 8, Part II, Chapter 6
Lilley, S. (1946). *Man, Machines and History.* Part II, Chapter 6. New York, International Publications (1966)

Iron and coal
Deane, P. Ref. 4, Chapter 7
Mantoux, P. Ref. 7, Part II, Chapter 3

Questions

What are the problems in using the terms science and technology with respect to the period of the Industrial Revolution? (see Refs. 3, 14, 19, 22, 23)

Points for discussion or essays

Discuss the proposition that the Scientific Revolution was a necessary precondition for the Industrial Revolution (see Refs. 1, 4—7)

Discuss the nature of the links, if any, between science and technical change in an industry of your choice during the Industrial Revolution in Britain. (see Refs. 1, 2, 12—17, Addendum)

'Science discovers, technology applies.' Comment on the validity of this commonly held view with regard to technological change in the Industrial Revolution in Britain. (see Refs. 1, 2, 12—17.)

'There is no contesting the reality of British industrial leadership in the eighteenth century, but it is conceivable that the industrial interests of British scientists were more a result than a cause of this pre-eminence' (C.C. Gillispie in Ref. 13). Discuss this view with particular regard to recent work in the social history of science. (see Refs. 13, 18—24.)

Chapter Two
Science and Industry in the Nineteenth Century

Although Britain was the first country to industrialize, its lead was comparatively short-lived and by the final quarter of the nineteenth century it had been caught, if not overtaken, by Germany and the USA. Thus, in considering the relationships between science, technology and industrial development in this later period our discussion must be international and include the new industrial nations. Also, during the nineteenth century and early twentieth century there were important changes in the nature of industry and the economy generally. Hobsbawm identifies four major changes:

> The first and in the long-run the most profound change was in the role of science in technology. The major technical advances of the second half of the nineteenth century were . . . essentially scientific. The second major change . . . simply consisted in the systematic extension of the factory system. The third major change consisted of the discovery that the largest potential market was to be found in the rising incomes of the mass of the working citizens in economically developed countries. The last major change was the increase in the scale of economic enterprise, the concentration of production and ownership, the rise of an economy composed of a handful of great lumps of rocks — trusts, monopolies — rather than a large number of pebbles.

In this chapter we shall be focusing on the first of these changes — the increasing importance of science in technology — and to help bring out the main issues we shall once again pose two questions:
1. How did science become more closely linked to industrial development?
2. What was the impact of this change on the organization and development of science?

After 1840, Britain's economic and industrial base broadened away from a reliance on textiles towards capital goods and other manufactures: it was in the period 1840—70 that Britain was said to be the 'workshop of the world'. In 1851, Britain, with half the population of France, was producing two-thirds of the world's coal and half its iron and cotton cloth. However, the major feature of the second half of the nineteenth century was the spread of industrial capitalism, particularly the growth and challenge to British supremacy of

13

Germany and the USA. The reasons for the rapid growth of the new industrial nations were complex and need to be weighed carefully in relation to specific industries and specific periods. Nonetheless it is possible to identify a number of general factors. The growth potential of the nascent industrial economies attracted investment, including capital from Britain. Industrializing later meant that the new industrial nations had a base in modern industries and had less capital tied up in old plant and out-dated technologies. These countries also showed greater willingness to use economic protection to shield nascent industries. Britain could have met this challenge head-on by modernizing its industrial base; instead, it sought the 'easier' path of further exploitation of its Empire. We would like to illustrate some of these general features and to begin to answer the first question posed above by discussing the development of the alkali sector of the chemical industry.

The alkali industry in the nineteenth century

The alkali industry (i.e. the manufacture of sodium carbonate and bicarbonate, soda ash and bleaching powder) was important in the early nineteenth century because of its links with washing and bleaching in the textile industry. Later it also became important in its own right as a user of sulfuric acid, and in soap and glass manufacture. Up to the 1820s, alkalis were obtained from natural sources, largely from burning seaweed, and like other branches of the chemical industry economic success depended largely on location, access to cheap raw materials and good organization – the industry was not very scientific. A method for the synthetic production of alkalis had been known since the 1780s; it became known as the Leblanc process and had been submitted to a competition organized by the French Academy. However, it was first commercially adopted and widely used in Britain in the 1820s. The reasons for the time-lag between invention (first technical sketch or model) and innovation (first commercial application) are complex, having to do with the economic effects of war, demand patterns, salt taxes, etc.

The chemistry of the Leblanc process was simple, if inelegant:

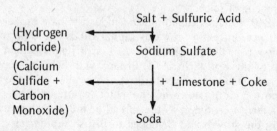

14

One writer recently described the process as 'an offence to chemist and manufacturer alike', to which we may add that it was a health hazard to the chemical worker and the population of the surrounding area. The process wasted sulfur and calcium, it produced large quantities of unburnt but grossly contaminated coal, and the poisonous hydrogen chloride gas, even when no longer vented into the atmosphere, still wasted valuable chlorine. However, during the nineteenth century the process saw many improvements. From 1836 it was possible to recover hydrogen chloride as hydrochloric acid, but as there was no market for the acid, the process was not widely used until the institution of the Alkali Acts in the 1860s. (The Alkali Acts restricted the emission of hydrogen chloride and were the first modern air pollution control measures in Britain; indeed the air pollution control agency in Britain is still called the Alkali Inspectorate.) In 1870 a more efficient method of chlorine recovery was introduced. This provided for the production of bleaching powder, and from 1887 it became possible to recover sulfur. The Leblanc industry remained concentrated in Britain and, in its 'Golden Age' from 1860–80, output rose three-fold, most went to the domestic market, but there was a growing export business.

However, from 1811 an alternative and more elegant method of alkali manufacture had been known:

$$\text{Ammonia + Salt + Carbon Dioxide}$$
$$\downarrow$$
$$\text{Soda + Ammonium Chloride}$$

The major problem with this process was the waste of expensive ammonia as ammonium chloride. The problem of recovering ammonia was solved by a Belgian, Ernest Solvay, in 1863. He devized a method of using a former waste product, quicklime, to yield free and recyclable ammonia. There were many problems in developing the process for large scale production, but by the 1870s Solvay-produced alkalis were able to undersell Leblanc by 20%. The reasons for the greater efficiency of the Solvay process are particularly significant. Whereas the Leblanc method was a batch process involving the mixing and heating of materials in vessels, Solvay's was a continuous or flow process. This meant labor costs were lower and the whole process could be better controlled. More importantly, the Solvay process used cheaper raw materials and very efficiently recycled and reused 'waste' products. It was the Solvay process that the new industrial nations adopted and soon contested the British supremacy.

The British Leblanc industry responded to this challenge in a number of ways: by increasing efficiency and process improvement; by concentration through the merging of companies to form the United Alkali Company, thus facilitating economies of scale; and entering into price fixing agreements with British Solvay producers.

The Leblanc industry maintained its position until 1895 when a new and cheaper electrolytic method of chlorine production was introduced. This hit the bleaching powder side of the Leblanc industry and led to British alkali production falling for the first time in the century. Exports of alkalis fell from £2.6 million in 1890 to £1.4 million in 1900. A crucial factor was the difference in the rate of the diffusion of Solvay technology between Germany and Britain. In 1882 Solvay accounted for 44% of German soda production, in 1887 the proportion was 75% and by 1900 over 90%. In Britain the percentage rose from 12 to 22 to 40 in the corresponding years, despite pioneering development work on the Solvay process by Mond in Lancashire. The relative backwardness of the alkali industry had effects in other sectors. For example, in chlorine production in 1904 only 18% of British production came from electrolytic plants compared with 65% in Germany and 100% in the USA. The last British Leblanc plant closed down in 1920, having survived until then by a series of commercial manoeuvres and because of the First World War limiting foreign competition.

This story shows a number of things. It shows the perils of industrial leadership — the technological changes in the British industry were slow in making themselves felt because the Leblanc process had been so well established and so much capital and skill had gone into it. It shows the growing importance of science in chemical technology and the importance of research and development. Process development and improvement was crucial to both the Leblanc and Solvay processes; indeed it was the small but incremental improvements in Leblanc technology that enabled it to continue as long as it did. Finally it shows not only the distinction between invention and innovation, but that between innovation and diffusion.

Industrial research and development

We would have liked to discuss in similar detail a number of other industrial sectors. For example, the case of the organic dyestuffs industry would have illustrated even more the significance of R & D, the need for technical virtuosity in research and production and marketing, the growing need for scientific manpower and the role of economic policy and tariffs. The case of the key sector of mechanical technology (machine tools, light engineering, etc.) would show the effects of large scale production and the extension of mechanization, the need for precision and standardization, the nature of mass production and the development of work study and 'scientific management'. The case of the electrical industry would show the emergence of several branches of industry all based on 'fundamental' scientific work carried out in the early nineteenth century by men like Volta,

Davy, Faraday, Wheatstone, etc. Each of these topics would reward further study and would reveal important points about the changing relationship between science and industry.

The main way in which science became more closely linked to production was through industrial R & D activity. Whatever the situation in the early nineteenth century, formal links between science and production were increasingly forged in the form of a distinct organization within the firm — the research and development laboratory. Moreover, the specialization and organization of inventive and innovative activity was not restricted to modern, science-related industries: it was also found in established industries like iron and steel. The R & D laboratory was required for a number of reasons, but not all of these apply to every industry. As we have already noted, technology generally became more science based. Increased mechanization and the growing complexity of production made it more difficult for operatives to initiate technical change. Quality control and standardization became more important and scientific. Finally, it became increasingly dangerous for firms to be left behind by technical change and in turn more profitable for them to invest in the exploration of new products and processes.

All this is not to suggest that all or even most inventive and innovative activity came from industrial R & D laboratories by the end of the nineteenth century. Taking industry as a whole the case was clearly otherwise. Rather, it is to point to a change that was underway and that became of fundamental importance to industrial development in the twentieth century.

The organization and development of science

The growing industrial role of science had a marked impact on the organization and development of science. These effects varied greatly between countries and at different times; thus the comparative study of changes in the position of science in, say, Britain, Germany and the USA deserves further reading and investigation. Nonetheless it is possible to pick out a number of general points.

The most important change was the emergence of science as a social institution on a significant scale and as a specialized, 'professional' activity. For example, being an analytical chemist became a specialized occupation, identified with a body of knowledge and practices, and seen to be socially useful. A second important feature was the growth of scientific and technical education, especially teaching and research in higher education where differences between countries were especially interesting. Thirdly, as economic and industrial goals became recognized as national goals, governments began to support and foster the development of science. Finally,

17

and somewhat strangely given the importance of the growing industrial role of science in generating these changes, the distinction between 'pure science' and 'applied science' became part of the ideology of science. This distinction served, and has continued to serve, a number of functions both within science and in the relationship between science and society, and is a topic well worth investigating further. Whilst the increased wealth, consequent upon industrialization, did lead to the support of science 'for its own sake', the main reason for the growth of university science was that in the long term and in unpredictable ways it was seen to be useful: not only in producing 'new knowledge', but in training manpower, developing new instruments and techniques, disseminating knowledge and providing facilities for work on specialized projects and contracts.

Reading

ESSENTIAL

1. Bernal, J.D. (1953). *Science and Industry in the Nineteenth Century.* London, Routledge Kegan Paul
   See Chapters 1 and 6. A good general introduction, other chapters discuss particular industries.
2. Freeman, C. (1974). *The Economics of Industrial Innovation.* London, Penguin
   See Chapters 2—4. These three chapters give brief historical accounts of the development of three science-related industries, but only read the sections relevant to the period 1840—1914
3. Beer, J.J. and Davies, W.D. (1963). 'Aspects of the professionalization of science.' *Daedalus,* **XCII**, 764—771 and 782—783. Good brief discussion of the emergence of industrial R & D laboratories.

RELATED

Industrial development 1800—1914
4. Cooper, C. (1971). 'Science, technology and development.' *Economic and Social Review (Dublin),* **2**, No. 2, Jan
   Addresses the problem of the limited growth of science and technology in developing countries through a discussion of views on the relationships between science, technology and production in nineteenth century Britain
5. Habakkuk, H.J. (1962). *American and British Technology in the Nineteenth Century.* Cambridge, Cambridge University Press
   Argues that labor shortages and high wages were a considerable stimulus to technical innovation in the US and largely account for its technological lead over Britain

6. Hobsbawm, E.J. (1968). *Industry and Empire.* London, Weidenfeld and Nicolson
   See especially Chapter 9; discusses Britain's relative backwardness in industrial development in the late ninteenth century
7. Jewkes, J., Sawers, D. and Stillerman, R. (1962). *The Sources of Invention.* London, Macmillan
   See Chapter 3. A pro-individualist/lone inventor history of technical change
8. Landes, D.S. (1969). *The Unbound Prometheus.* Cambridge, Cambridge University Press
   See especially Chapter 5 'Short breath and second wind'; good discussion of German industrial development again emphasizing technological change
9. Saul, S.B. (1970). *Technological Change: The United States and Britain in the Nineteenth Century.* New York, University Paperbacks
   A set of readings based on Habakkuk's thesis
10. Schmookler, J. (1960). 'The economic sources of inventive activity.' *Journal of Economic History,* March, 1–20. Or in *The Economics of Technical Change,* 117–137. Ed. N. Rosenberg. London, Penguin (1971)
    Uses patent data to show that 'technological progress is intimately dependent on economic phenomena'

ADDENDUM: DEVELOPMENT OF SPECIFIC INDUSTRIES

Chemicals
11. Beer, J.J. (1958). 'Coal tar dye manufacture and the origins of the modern industrial research laboratory.' *Isis,* **49**, 123–131
    Discusses the technical development of the industry with particular reference to Germany
12. Haber, L. (1957). *The Chemical Industry During the Nineteenth Century.* Oxford, Oxford University Press
    Very detailed discussions of all the main branches of the industry; *the* standard work
13. Richardson, H.J. (1962). 'The development of the British dyestuffs industry before 1939.' *Scottish Journal of Political Economy,* **9**, 110–129
14. Williams, T.I. (1972). *The Chemical Industry.* London, E.P. Publishing
    Recently reprinted as an Open University set book, but suffers from comparison with Haber

Electricals
15. Cardwell, D.S.L. (1972). *Technology, Science and History.* London, Heinemann
    See especially Chapter 5 on communications technologies

16. Hughes, T.P. (1962). 'The British electrical industry lag.'
Technology and Culture, 3, 27–44
Discusses classic problem of Britain's relative backwardness in
certain aspects of electrical technology
17. Kieve, J.L. (1973). *The Electric Telegraph – a social and
economic history*. Newton Abbott, David and Charles
The most detailed recent account
18. MacLauren, W.R. (1974). *The Rise of the Electrical Industry in
the Nineteenth Century*. New York, Arno
Probably the best general account

Machines
19. Floud, R. (1976). *The British Machine-Tool Industry 1850–1914*.
Cambridge, Cambridge University Press
Claims to be the first history of this key sector of British industry.
20. Lilley, S. (1946). *Men, Machines and History*. New York, Inter-
national Publications (1966)
Advances technological determinist arguments
21. Rosenberg, N. (1963). 'Technological Change in the Machine
Tool industry 1840–1910.' *Journal of Economic History*, **XXIII**
Good reference to start with

The organization of science
22. Armytage, W.H.G. (1965). *The Rise of the Technocrats – a social
history*. London, Routledge Kegan Paul
Encyclopaedic, but very useful for that reason
23. Ashby, E. (1958). *Technology and the Academics*. London,
Macmillan
Very readable discussion of the ecology of universities in the
eighteenth and nineteenth centuries
24. Ben-David, J. (1971). *The Scientists Role in Society – A
comparative study*. Englewood Cliffs, N.J., Prentice Hall
Has quickly become a standard work, but often ignores wider
social changes and the changing nature of science itself
25. Mendelsohn, E. (1964). 'The emergence of science as a profession
in nineteenth century Europe.' In *The Management of Scientists*.
Ed. K. Hill. Boston, Mass., Beacon
Suggests professionalization arose out of links with technology,
education and industrial R & D laboratories

Britain
26. Berman, M. (1975). ' "Hegemony" and the amateur tradition in
British science.' *Journal of Social History*, No. 1, 30–50
Good discussion of the 'reluctance' of nineteenth century British
science to 'professionalize'

27. Cardwell, D.S.L. (1972). *The Organization of Science in England.* London, Heinemann
    The standard work, but is mainly about applied science and technical education
28. Musgrave, P.W. (1967). *Technical Change, the Labour Force and Education — A study of the British and German iron and steel industries 1860–1964.* Oxford, Pergamon
    In spite of the title, mainly the history of technical education, with good comparative studies

France
29. Gilpin, R. (1968). *France in the Age of the Scientific State.* Princeton, N.J., Princeton University Press
    Mainly on the twentieth century, but has some sections on the nineteenth century by way of historical introduction

Germany
30. Ben-David, J. and Zloczower, A. (1972). 'The growth of institutionalized science in Germany.' In *Sociology of Science,* 45–59. Ed. B. Barnes. London, Penguin
    Discusses how the 'utility' of science came to be perceived

The United States of America
31. Birr, K.A. (1966). 'Science in American industry.' In *Science and Society in the United States,* 35–80. Ed. D.D. Van Tassel and M.G. Hall. Homewood, Illinois, Dorsey Press
    Discusses the place of science in key industries
32. Daniels, G.H. (1967). 'The pure-science ideal and democratic culture.' *Science,* **156,** 30 June, 1699–1705
    Discusses the problems of the 'autonomy' of the emergent profession

Questions

How did the industrialization of *either* Germany *or* the USA with regard to technology compare: (a) with that of Britain in the Industrial Revolution and (b) with the position of Britain in the final quarter of the nineteenth century? (see Refs. 1, 3, 5–10.)

Points for discussion or essays

'Science discovers, technology applies'. Discuss the validity of this model of technical change with regard to two branches of science *or* two areas of technological development in the period 1840–1914. (See Refs. 1, 2, 5, 7, 9, 11–19.)

Describe and discuss the reasons for the emergence of industrial R & D in the late nineteenth century. Illustrate your answer with reference to at least two industrial sectors. (See Refs. 1–3, 7, 10, 11–19)

'In the late 1860s the German dyestuffs industry was still small, dispersed and largely imitative. Scarcely a decade later . . . it held about half of the world market; by the turn of the century, its share was around 90%.' Discuss the reasons for Germany's success and Britain's failure in developing this new science-based industry. (See Refs. 2, 11–14, 25, 27.)

Compare and contrast the institutionalization and organization of science in the late nineteenth century in *two* of the following countries: Britain; France; Germany; the USA (See refs. 1, 3, 22–32.)

The distinction between 'pure science' and 'applied science' arose during the nineteenth century. Discuss the origins of this distinction and the interests it might have served. Is the distinction a valid or useful one, either historically or contemporarily? (See refs. 2, 23–28, 32.)

Chapter Three
Science, Technology and Modern War

It is impossible to ignore the close involvement of contemporary science and technology with war and the military. Indeed, the influence of the military on science and technology is out of all proportion to the place of the military in society generally.

> While military expenditures represent less than 6 % of the world's GNP, they engage an estimated 25% of the world's scientific talent, and command 40% of all public and private expenditure for R & D.

This close involvement of science and technology with war and the military is not new. However, there is little doubt that industrialization did alter the character of warfare and its relationship with science and technology. Wars became not only battles between armies, but also 'battles' between whole societies involving the mobilization of virtually every facet of society. In other words, war became 'total' war. In the nineteenth century it was technologies first developed for civilian purposes that most influenced the nature and conduct of wars, these being principally the railway, the electric telegraph and the steamship. While these technologies were also important in the conduct of the First World War, during that war a number of specialized military technologies were developed which were crucial in the conduct of the Second World War, i.e. the tank, military combat aircraft, very large warships, etc. Also in both World Wars science and scientists were increasingly mobilized to the war effort and in the Second World War this mobilization led to striking developments — radar, operations research, new explosives and, of course, the atomic bomb.

Probably the most significant happening in the world since 1945 has been the development, through atomic and nuclear weapons, of the capability in a future war of the annihilation of the whole of mankind and most other forms of life. Yet, writing in 1948, P.M.S. Blackett argued that the advent of the atomic bomb had *not* revolutionized warfare. He argued, firstly, that there were very few situations in which atomic weapons could be used; and secondly, that experience in the Second World War had shown the bombing of industrial and civilian targets to be ineffective. Blackett was probably right at the time, but clearly he did not, and probably could not, foresee that the military would learn the lesson from the Second

World War that deliberate mobilization of science and technology could lead to spectacular and rapid advances in weapons technology and performance.

Building on the basis of radar, German rocket technology and the first atomic device, 'weapons' have evolved considerably. They have passed from the vulnerable B29 bomber carrying a single atomic bomb of 0.02 megatons* to the invulnerable intercontinental ballistic missile, capable of travelling thousands of miles, of hitting targets to within an accuracy of one mile, of carrying single or multiple warheads of up to 50 megatons and housed in readiness in undetectable nuclear submarines at the bottom of the ocean or in case-hardened silos on the US prairies or Russian steppes. These developments, mostly 'created by modern science and technology', have had momentous implications for humanity and, incidentally (and really much less importantly), momentous implications for science and technology. The central questions for this topic are, therefore:

How has the relationship between science, technology and war developed since the Second World War?

What have been the main determinants and consequences of the changes in this relationship?

We can consider the first question under five headings:

(i)   The possibility of the annihilation of the human race.
(ii)   The changed nature of warfare and international relations.
(iii) The enormous waste of resources.
(iv)   The arms race and its relation to security.
(v)   The creation of a military—industrial—scientific complex.

The possibility of the annihilation of the human race

The first point is made very simply. In 1965 Melman estimated that with 10% penetration with bombers and 25% penetration with missiles the USA had the capacity to destroy the main Russian population centers *220 times* over. This capacity is known among nuclear strategists as 'overkill'. Progress in this field being what it is, the situation today is probably that the USA has sufficient nuclear weapons to kill most of the world's population 15 times over. If we add this to an equivalent capacity held by the USSR (which is being conservative) and include the potential of other powers it is likely that the world's nuclear stockpile has the potential to destroy the world's population *at least 30 times* over. Even then this only takes

---

*A bomb of 1 megaton has an explosive power equivalent to 1 million times that of 1 ton of TNT.

into account the direct destructive effects and ignores the longer term impact of radioactive fall-out and the total breakdown in civilization that would occur.

The changed nature of warfare and international relations

The second feature of the relationship between science, technology and war is that this enormous increase in destructive potential has altered the nature of international relations and the nature of any future war. Clausewitz's classical definition of war as the pursuit of diplomatic ends by other means simply does not hold any more between the great powers. The advances in weapons technology have meant that effective defense against attack is virtually impossible and that a surprise attack attempting to knock out all of an enemy's offensive weapons is very unlikely to succeed. It is possible to argue that war has always been immoral, but previously it could be seen to be rational in terms of economic, political or territorial objectives. War is now irrational as well as immoral, but this alone will not stop it happening. The contemporary position was summed up in 1966 by Buchan:

> One of the central facts of international politics today is that the participants in the central balance of power, whether super states or minor allies, do not feel that they have the liberty of action to pursue conflicts . . . to the length of war. It is only countries outside the main East—West balance of power, or on the fringe of it, who can permit themselves the luxury of fighting over territory, e.g. India—Pakistan, Israel—Arab States.

The recent conflicts in the Middle East well illustrate what happens on the fringe. Firstly, Clausewitz still holds as shown by the territorial changes that have accompanied each war. Secondly, the great powers become involved through backing one side or the other, but they are never close enough for a direct confrontation (the Cuban missile crisis in 1962 being the frightening exception that proves the rule). Thirdly, the great powers act as suppliers of arms and equipment, the sales of which help to underwrite the development costs of expensive weapons and, in the West at least, can give weapons development a greater economic justification.

The enormous waste of resources

The third important feature is the enormous waste of resources. In the major powers 5—10% of the Gross National Product is spent on defense, compared with less than 1% on aid for developing countries. On the most simple interpretation, resources are wasted because of the tremendous, unnecessary overkill. On a more radical interpretation we can ask what kind of society would devote resources to the construction of one polaris submarine with 16 intercontinental ballistic missiles that could otherwise provide 331 elementary schools, or 6811 hospital beds, or 13 723 low-income houses?

The Arms Race and its relation to security

The fourth point is that the Arms Race which increases the power of weapons to unbelievable proportions, and which consumes vast resources, *does not* increase the security of the nations involved. In fact, the security of these nations has probably diminished.

> Both sides in the arms race are thus confronted by the dilemma of steadily increasing military power and steadily decreasing national security. It is our considered professional judgement that this dilemma has no technical solution. If the great powers continue to look for solutions in the area of science and technology only, the result will be to worsen the situation. The clearly predictable course of the arms race is a steady open spiral downward into oblivion (Weisner and York).

Moreover, the recent development of the long-range cruise missile threatens to further destabilize the strategic balance.

The creation of a military—industrial—scientific complex

The fifth important feature of the development of the relationship between science, technology and war is the creation of a military—industrial (—scientific) complex (MIC). The MIC can best be defined as a coalition of certain industrial interests: the military, big science and technology, and others who profit from the proliferation of war and have an interest in preparations for such an eventuality. The history of MICs is not well documented, but it seems probable that they have always existed, e.g. medieval armorers; Krupps in pre-war Germany. What is new today is, firstly, their size and power and, secondly, the central involvement of scientists and technologists in them. Most is known about the MIC in the USA and our discussion will reflect this. It should be stressed, however, that similar 'complexes' exist in other countries such as the USSR, China, and of course, Britain and France.

The potential importance of a military—industrial complex was seen by US industrialists as early as the Second World War. It has been argued, therefore, that the huge arms expenditure of the 1950s and 1960s and the creation of an MIC were developed to stave off economic depression by stimulating economic demand. This is the theory of a 'permanent arms economy' which will be discussed later.

The concept of the military—industrial complex first came to public awareness in the USA in President Eisenhower's valedictory speech in 1961:

> This conjunction of an immense military establishment and a large arms industry is new in the American experience . . . In the councils of government one must guard against the acquisition of unwarranted influence, whether sought or unsought, by the MIC. The potential for the disastrous use of misplaced power exists and will persist . . . . Akin to, and largely responsible for, this has been the technological revolution . . . . The prospect of domination of the nation's scholars by Federal employment, project allocation and the power of money is ever present but there is an equal and opposite danger that public policy could itself become the captive of a scientific—technological elite.

Since 1961 a great deal has been learnt about the MIC in the USA; we want to look briefly at its most important features and some of their consequences.

The first important characteristic of the MIC is its size and the range of interests involved in and dependent upon military budgets. In the 1960s US military budgets ran to the order of $70—80 billion; with space adding another $4—7 billion, this was approximately 50% of total federal government spending or $400 for every man, woman and child in the country. In all, 10% of the US labor force had become directly dependent on the military—industrial economy for its employment and income. Within the MIC there was a high degree of concentration of resources. In 1968 the top 25 industrial contractors of the Department of Defense (DOD) accounted for 46% of DOD expenditures, the top 100 contractors for 66%; whereas in total there were 22 500 contracting companies. There also grew up an important geopolitical lobby within the US Congress, with politicians pressing for military spending in their constituencies; in 1968 10 states received 60% of DOD expenditures. The involvement of universities is shown by the fact that in 1968 MIT was the 54th largest DOD contractor, whilst Johns Hopkins University was 85th, and in all $71 million of DOD monies were channelled to universities.

The second feature of the MIC is its overt political role. The scale of operations and expenditures described above required a *raison d'etre.* This was provided by elaborate fabrications of external threats posed by communism, Soviet aspirations, etc. In terms of technology it was expressed in the 1950s by the 'Bomber Gap' and in the 1960s by the 'Missile Gap', both of which have been shown to be imaginary. This whole mentality was sometimes given a false 'scientific' credence by certain strategy analysts and war gamers, and their use of terms such as 'minimum deterrent', 'first strike capability' and 'damage limitation'. The 'Gap' notions were exacerbated by the pathological secrecy of the USSR about its military intentions and resources, although this was understandable given that it wanted to appear stronger than it really was. More recently, sophisticated spy technology (including space satellites) and the detente between the USA and the USSR have diminished the importance of such posturing. However, fears of the other side's technological development are still being used to support new weapons programs, e.g. control of the sea bed and the recent controversy over Soviet military R & D.

A third important feature of the MIC is that there grew up a number of large companies almost totally dependent on government defense expenditures; this is referred to as the 'locked-in relationship'. Such a situation creates great problems in public accountability, the power of private companies and the geographical and commercial constituencies thereby created. A typical result has been the prevalence of abortive and costly new weapons projects: Danhof found that 'costs in excess of original contractual estimates of from 300 to 700%' have been typical. These problems are inevitable given that no price or cost precedents exist in radically new technology and that the government is the sole customer. They have been compounded, however, by corruption and pork-barreling between Congress, DOD and contractors.

The fourth aspect of the MIC, which we have already touched on, has been the involvement of 'academic science' with this coalition. The USA has never developed machinery to fund university research through quasi-independent bodies such as the UGC and Research Councils in Britain and those that exist in most other industrial countries. The US National Science Foundation created in 1950 to fulfil this role has always been inadequately funded so that US scientists have had to seek funds from wherever they were available. In essence, the US scientific community has never severed the umbilical cord between itself and the military created in the Second World War.

Since the late 1960s, however, the military—industrial—scientific complex has been on the defensive, at least within the USA. Overall military related budgets, as a percentage of total US Federal Government spending, fell from 50% in 1963 to 35% in 1973. Similarly, military R & D, as a percentage of total federal R & D, fell from

71% in 1961 to 48% in 1971. The reasons for this cutback are manifold. They include the phasing-out of direct US involvement in Vietnam, Nixon's policies of cutting government spending, various Congressional moves to stop waste in the DOD (e.g. the work of Senator William Proxmire and the Senate Sub-Committee he chaired) and the public's growing hostility to big technology projects such as the Supersonic Transport, the Anti-Ballistic Missile scheme, and manned space flight. These cutbacks have created severe problems for many of the 'locked-in' companies and created unemployment amongst scientists and technologists in certain sectors. Yet still the overkill potential continues to grow, international relations remain under the spectre of total annihilation, the arms race continues and the military—industrial—scientific complex is far from defunct.

Causes of the Arms Race

The story of the arms race and the growth of the MIC present grounds for considerable disquiet. Yet to describe their terrifying evolution is not enough. One must go further and consider how this situation came about and what steps might be taken to diminish or remove the threat of a nuclear holocaust. The first step in such an analysis must be to consider the causes of the arms race, for it might be argued that only when one has some understanding of these can one begin to formulate solutions.

There are a number of theories on the causes of the arms race; however, we shall draw your attention to the three most important and influential. The first of these is the Marxist thesis of Baran and Sweezy. This postulates that the Cold War, the arms race and the growth of the MIC are devices whereby modern industrial capitalism attempts to absorb its surplus production, thereby controlling the cyclical economic depressions and also defending (and furthering) overseas economic interests. A second theory is that advanced by Buchan. This sees the arms race as developing from the nature of international relations between the USA and the USSR, especially with regard to changes in the balance of power, the problem of security and the influence on these of modern strategic thinking, particularly deterrence theory. The final view is that developments in weapons science and technology are the main determinants of the arms race. Thus military R & D and the extension of technical possibilities, rather than responding to the needs of the military, industry or government, are seen to have their own dynamic. The full articulation and discussion of these theories will require further reading and investigation; indeed, such an undertaking is crucial to any real understanding of the changing relationships between science, technology and warfare.

When approached from the perspective of the causes of the arms race, the problem of arms control and disarmament is perhaps rather more complex and far-reaching than is often supposed, a point that is vividly illustrated by the agreements on arms control negotiated to date.

The Partial Test Ban Treaty (PTBT) signed in 1963 has been described as the 'first international clean air act', for although it halted atmospheric tests (thereby reducing atmospheric radiation levels), it did little to halt the arms race. Since the treaty was signed there have been more underground tests than there were total tests beforehand. The 1968 Nuclear Non-Proliferation Treaty (NNPT) was designed to prevent the emergence of more 'nuclear nations'; however, few countries ratified the treaty and after the explosion of the Indian nuclear device in 1974, the chances of preventing proliferation do not look good. The problem is, of course, exacerbated by the spread of nuclear power plants and the difficulties of ensuring nuclear waste is not diverted to weapons programs. The Strategic Arms Limitation Talks (SALT) which began in 1969 have had some success in limiting defensive weapons — anti-ballistic missiles (ABM) — and have set quantitative ceilings for numbers of nuclear warheads. However, many now feel that a quantitative arms race will simply be superceded by a qualitative one. None of these measures seem to have been particularly effective in halting the arms race, so there are perhaps grounds for some cynicism, yet perhaps one must also accept that anything done to slow down the arms race and make nuclear war less likely is to be welcomed.

Reading

ESSENTIAL

1. Buchan, A. (1966). *War in Modern Society.* London, Watts; London, Fontana (1968)
   See Chapters 2 and 4—6. Famous writer on modern warfare, discusses how the nature of post-war international relations has led to the arms race. Later chapters look at problems of arms control.
2. Baran, P.A. and Sweezy, P.M. (1966). *Monopoly Capital.* New York, Monthly Review Press; London, Penguin (1968)
   See Chapter 7. Classic statement of the theory of the permanent arms economy.
3. Clarke, R. (1972). *The Science of War and Peace.* New York, McGraw-Hill
   See Chapter 5. Argues that science and technology are the determinants of the arms race
4. Young, E. (1972). *Farewell to Arms Control.* London, Penguin

See Chapters 6–8 and 11. Best readily available account of arms control agreements, but does not contain details of most recent developments with SALT

FURTHER

The Arms Race
5. Barnaby, F. (1971). *The Nuclear Future.* Fabian Tract 394. London, Fabian Society
   Very good introduction, the most accessible and wide-ranging discussion and a good place to begin your reading
6. Barnaby, F. (1975). 'Will the cruise missile torpedo SALT.' *New Scientist*, 18/25 December, 679–681
7. Kidron, M. (1970). *Western Capitalism Since the War.* London, Penguin
   Marxist account. Argues that the permanent arms economy has been responsible for the 'survival' of modern capitalism, not easy going but worth persevering
8. Sivard, R.L. (1975). 'Let them eat bullets.' *Bulletin of the Atomic Scientists*, **31**, April, 6–10
   Attempts to estimate world spending on armaments and what else could be done with the resources, especially in terms of problems facing developing countries.
9. Weisner, J. and York, H. (1964). 'National Security and the Nuclear Test Ban.' *Scientific American*, April
   Famous article which concludes that by the criterion of increasing national security the arms race is self-defeating
10. York, H. (1969). 'Military Technology and national security.' *Scientific American*, August, 17–29
    Makes the same points as the 1964 article with Weisner, except with regard to the ABM
11. York, H. (1970). *Race to Oblivion.* New York, Simon and Schuster
    Argues that the US has been involved in a number of arms races and that each has been illusory

The military–industrial complex
12. Erikson, J. (1971). 'The Military–Industrial Complex. *Science Studies*, **1**, 225–233
    Essay review of the major books on the MIC published in 1970; agrees with most of the books that the political control of the MIC is the main issue
13. Lens, S. (1971). *The Military–Industrial Complex.* Kahn and Averill
    Standard work; argues that the development of the MIC is linked to USA expansionist aims

14. Lewin, L. (1968). *Report from Iron Mountain: on the possibility and desirability of peace.* London, Penguin
    Purported to be an official report showing that 'peace' was an unnacceptable policy alternative for the US
15. Melman, S. (1972). 'Who Needs a War Economy.' *The Nation*, **215**, 487–488
    Sees the war economy as 'Pentagon Capitalism' — nicely identifies those with vested interests in the maintenance of the war economy.
16. Proxmire, W. (1970). *Report from the Wasteland.* New York, Praeger
    Mainly concerned with the control of the MIC, particularly in relation to contracts and cost overruns.
17. Werskey, G. (1973). *War and Society A301.* Unit 31 'Science and war in the twentieth century'. Milton Keynes, Open University Press
    Discusses the MIC, the permanent arms economy and the scientization of war; would be a good introduction

Disarmament
18. Barnaby, F. (1975). *Nuclear Disarmament or Nuclear War.* SPIRI
    Argues the case for disarmament being essential
19. Epstein, W. (1975). 'The outlook for disarmament.' In *The Dynamics of the Arms Race,* 104–115. Ed. D. Carlton and C. Schaerf. London, Croom Helm
    Reviews disarmament measures to date and looks at future prospects
20. Noel Baker, P. (1960). *The Arms Race: A programme for world disarmament.* London, Calder
    An optimistic assessment written in 1960, but still makes for interesting reading

Proliferation of nuclear weapons
21. Barnaby, F. (1975). *Preventing Nuclear Weapon Proliferation.* SPIRI
    A very thorough discussion
22. Collingridge, D. and Gutteridge, W. (1975). *Problems of Disarmament and the Arms Race.* University of Leeds, Siscon
    Very useful teaching unit on disarmament, especially the case studies on India and the Middle East
23. Epstein, W. (1975). 'The proliferation of nuclear weapons.' *Scientific American,* April, 18–33
    Discusses nuclear proliferation in the context of the Indian 'peaceful' nuclear explosion
24. Halstead, T. (1975). 'The spread of nuclear weapons — is the dam to burst?' *Bulletin of the Atomic Scientists,* **31**, May, 8–11
    Discusses possible improvements in Non-Proliferation Treaty

25. Beaton, L. (1966). *Must the Bomb Spread?* London, Penguin
    A pessimistic view, sees little hope of preventing more and more
    countries acquiring the bomb

Questions

What is meant by the term 'military—industrial complex?
What is the validity of extending the term to the 'military—
industrial—scientific complex'? (See Refs. 12—17.)

Have there been any meaningful effective steps taken to
control nuclear weapons and effect nuclear disarmament?
Has the likelihood of achieving arms control and disarmament
increased, diminished or remained unchanged in the past ten
years? (See Refs. 1, 4, 18—20.)

Points for discussion or essays

Describe and discuss the most important changes in the
relationship between science, technology and war since 1945.
Does the term 'scientization of war' adequately describe the
main features of the period? (See Refs. 1, 5, 6, 8, 9—11.)

Compare, contrast and evaluate three views on the causes of
the arms race. (See Refs. 1—3, 7, 11, 15, 17.)

'There is no technical solution to the dilemma of the steady
decrease in our national security that has for more than
twenty years accompanied the steady increase in our military
power' (Herbert F. York). Comment on this opinion of the
US security position. (See Refs. 4—6, 9—11.)

'A world of nuclear powers'. Discuss. (See Refs. 1, 4, 21—25.)

Chapter Four
Science, Technology and
Modern Industry

In capitalist countries, a large volume of government spending and government management of the economy are an integral part of the economic system. This has not always been the case. Government spending in most western countries now accounts for about 25% of the GNP*, whereas in 1929 it only took about 2% of the GNP. It is this change that has given rise to the concept of a 'mixed economy', with complementary private and public sectors. It grew out of the economic depression and large scale unemployment of the 1930s, and the revision of economic theory by John Maynard Keynes. Keynesian theory and its derivatives postulate that large and active public spending is needed in an advanced capitalist economy to regulate and stabilize demand, by keeping investment in line with saving and consumption in order to avoid inflation or unemployment, or repeated cycles of both. An associated change occurred in the relation of military spending to public expenditure as a whole. In the USA in the early 1930s military expenditure accounted for 10–15% of public spending, whereas in the early 1960s it accounted for 55–60%. From this the American economist J.K. Galbraith has argued:

> If a large public sector of the economy, supported by personal and corporate income taxation, is the fulcrum for the regulation of demand, plainly military expenditures are the pivot on which the fulcrum rests.

Galbraith is referring mainly to the USA, the largest modern capitalist economy. How accurate his point would be for other capitalist countries is debatable.

High military spending, as we saw in the last chapter, is dangerous and wasteful, yet, if it is the 'pivot' on which the largest capitalist economy is balanced, it will be difficult to abolish. There are two opposing views on the feasibility of running down military spending. The first argues that it would be comparatively straightforward to transfer public spending to more socially desirable areas and objectives, or to cut taxes drastically. The second argues that running down military spending would lead to the collapse of modern capitalist economy through lack of demand and underconsumption. Galbraith takes an intermediary position:

*GNP = Gross National Product

34

One cannot replace the spending for armaments with private outlays for consumption and investment, such as would be encouraged by a massive reduction in taxes. The regulation of aggregate demand requires that the public sector of the economy be large . . . .

While all expenditure, whether for arms or old age pensions or air pollution, add to demand, not all play the same role in underwriting technology. Military spending, we have seen, is highly serviceable in this regard. . . . 'A drastic reduction in weapons competition following a general release from the commitment to the Cold War would be sharply in conflict with the needs of the industrial system. But these needs do not have to be met by weapons. Anything that is roughly equivalent in scale and technical complexity will serve'.

Thus, as we can see, Galbraith places technology at the forefront of his view of the Modern Industrial State.

In looking at the relationship between industrial development, technical change and science in the modern period, we shall take as our framework the ideas of J.K. Galbraith. In this chapter we shall consider his views on the giant corporation and technical innovation and, in the next, his views on government support of science and technology. According to Galbraith, the relationships between the economy, technology and science since the Second World War have been dominated by the 'imperatives of technology': that is, technology and technical change define the form of economic organization, the direction of social change and the nature of the development of science.

Technological change and the giant corporation

Galbraith, like some other contemporary economists, sees the giant corporation as the dominant institution of the modern industrial order. He argues that increasingly sophisticated and expensive technology defines 'both the needs and opportunity for the large business corporation'. By this he means that only the giant corporations can: (1) provide the necessary scale of capital investments; (2) absorb the risks of long lead-times and inflexible production; (3) provide the management organization and market planning to cope with these risks; (4) provide the requisite specialized manpower and technical skills. Galbraith sees, therefore, large firms and planning as the main consequences of modern technology and technical change. Only large firms and corporations are able to cope with modern technology, and are hence the main sources of invention and innovation.

Many people still think of science as it appeared to be in the nineteenth century, as the product of individual efforts of men of genius, instead of, as it now is, a highly organized new profession closely linked with industry and government . . . It is almost as difficult in an age of vast engineering and chemical factories, each furnished with its own research department, to recall the intimate tradition and practical character of the old workshops and forges from which the modern giants descended.

This view is not unchallenged. Many people argue that the small firms and the lone inventor still make a very significant contribution to technical innovation.

Small firms have often made very major innovations, either because large firms have not had effective methods of evaluating and implementing radical proposals, or because major innovations often involve great uncertainties so that even the best managed of large firms may let important opportunities slip through their fingers.

Recent examples of important innovations made by small firms include Xerography, polaroid film and big scientific computers.

Firm size and industrial innovation

The empirical evidence on this matter of firm size and innovation has to be interpreted carefully. Statistics would seem to confirm the supposed links between R & D and large firms. The percentage of large firms undertaking R & D is higher than the percentage of small firms. Furthermore, up to employment levels of 5000, larger firms spend a higher proportion of their sales on R & D than the smaller firms that perform R & D. Finally, when industrial firms are ranked by the size of R & D programs, the first 20 account for at least half of industrial R & D in most advanced Western countries; R & D is certainly more concentrated in large firms than the volume of production, or of employment.

However, this does not mean that there are only obvious advantages in being a large firm. In some industrial sectors (electronics, instruments), there are very research intensive small firms. In the USA, the output of patents (i.e. inventions) is not higher in bigger firms relative to employment levels and sales; it may be that small firms are able to innovate without formal, full-time R & D departments. In most US industries the percentage of sales spent on R & D does not increase amongst the very largest firms.

Generalizations are difficult to make because there are big differences between industrial sectors in the nature and importance of industrial innovation: small firms can successfully develop scientific instruments, but not nuclear reactors; electronics firms can make more use of new science than firms making furniture.

From the point of view of organization and management, there is a continuing discussion of the relative advantages and disadvantages of firm size in technical innovation. On the one hand, it is argued that large firms are able: 1. to spread risks by undertaking more and a wider selection of projects; 2. to employ and utilize highly specialized skills; 3. to operate on a large scale and with greater sophistication; 4. to have their own fundamental research laboratories; and 5. to afford management and market planning techniques. On the other hand, small firms are better able: 1. to make more rapid decisions and act upon them; 2. to avoid vested interests in the firm; 3. to encourage personal commitment to and identification with projects; and 4. to 'couple' the activities of research—development—production—marketing more effectively. For some observers 'both large and small firms play essential roles in the process of technological innovation and . . . these roles are complementary, interdependent and ever-changing.'

Conditions for successful industrial innovation

According to Galbraith, the second main consequence of the 'imperatives of technology' is planning. There are two aspects of planning: firstly, planning in the giant corporation in relation to technology, and secondly, government planning of the economy and social system as a whole. Galbraith sees the former as most important and as determining the development of the latter:

> From the time and capital that must be committed, the inflexibility of this commitment, the needs of large organizations and the problems of market performance under conditions of advanced technology comes the necessity for planning.

Galbraith illustrates the importance of planning in modern industrial society by reference to the automobile industry. A new model takes approximately five years to develop from conception and design to final production. The final product has anything from 1000 to 10 000 standardized components and its actual assembly involves investment of enormous amounts of capital in plant and tooling and the commitment of a large labor force. The giant motor corporation, so Galbraith argues, attempts to reduce the risks inherent in a process of this scale and complexity by planning; that is by market research, controlling retail outlets, advertizing, stopping production of competing models, etc. This is 'planning' in the first sense described above and is seen by Galbraith to derive from the 'imperatives of technology', i.e. complexity, costs, inflexibility, scale, time, etc. The role of government 'planning' in relation to automobile production is to ensure the viability of the industry as a whole. This it does by maintaining and increasing consumption expenditures, and ensuring an adequate road system and fuel supplies.

According to Galbraith, market planning by the giant corporations attempt in its most direct form to replace consumer sovereignty by producer sovereignty. Markets and sales are planned and manipulated through market research, retail control, advertizing, etc. to the requirements of the producer and the capabilities of his technology. There is another form of market planning only recently recognized by Galbraith in which firms anticipate and prepare for market uncertainties, but do not attempt the direct control or influence described above. It is, however, in the first stronger sense that Galbraith believes planning to be important in the giant corporation.

Galbraith's elegant account of industrial planning glosses over three important and inter-related questions that are crucial to the case he wishes to make. Firstly, to what extent can firms plan, predict and control R & D and technical innovation? Secondly, to what extent can they plan and predict markets? Thirdly, can firms achieve high probabilities of both technical and market success?

The first problem in answering these questions is that though sophisticated notions of 'technological forecasting' and of 'project selection' have been very fashionable in R & D management literature, there is little evidence that they have been extensively, let alone successfully, used in industrial firms. Studies of R & D management show that managers are more confident of their ability to predict project costs than market trends, but R & D managers are not in fact any good at all at predicting project costs! The weight of evidence from empirical innovation studies suggests that success in technical innovation is most closely related to meeting customer needs and to knowledge of the market. A recent study of successful and unsuccessful innovations in the chemical and scientific instruments industries concluded:

Successful innovations : have fewer after-sales problems
: need less adaptation by users
: have fewer technical 'bugs' in production
: need fewer modifications resulting from user experience after commercial sales
: have fewer unsuspected adjustments in production

than unsuccessful innovations.

Successful innovating firms : understand user requirements better
: employ greater sales effort
: devote more effort to educating users
: give more publicity to the innovation

than unsuccessful firms.

These restatements of customer sovereignty need to be qualified in two ways. Firstly, where customer sovereignty can be shown to prevail, it is nonetheless the case that the customer only has a certain range of choice, and that this might not be complete. Secondly, about 90% of total industrial R & D is spent on capital and intermediate goods, and only 10% on consumer durables, gadgets and goods. In other words, the typical situation is not of the giant corporation devoting its huge research facilities to produce a new, sexy, striped toothpaste to sell to individual, technically ignorant customers. Instead, it is of the giant corporation often competing to sell materials, machines, etc., to technically sophisticated organizations, who are often giant corporations themselves. Moreover, in consumer goods one needs to distinguish 'innovations' that incorporate new knowledge, materials and techniques and 'differentiated products' made to be different ('new') by superficial and trivial changes. Most of Galbraith's examples are of consumer goods, where his criticisms of 'producer sovereignty' may carry more weight, given that 'product development' often has little to do with science and technology.

However, this is not always the case. The pharmaceutical industry is one of the most research intensive of all industries, yet the customer (either patient or doctor) is often not in a position to evaluate the effectiveness of new pharmaceutical products. It is perhaps for this reason that this industry continues to be a subject of intense public scrutiny and debate.

In conclusion, it would appear that the 'imperatives of technology' are not alone responsible for the dominance of the giant corporation and planning in the modern industrial state. There are strong grounds for arguing that the modern capitalist economy is better than Galbraith thinks at getting useful new technology and production through the producers' goods sector.

Reading

ESSENTIAL

1. Galbraith, J.K. (1966). *The New Industrial State*. 2nd edn. London, Penguin (1974)
   See Chapters 1–4 and 7. On the importance of the 'imperatives of modern technology'.
2. Jewkes, J. *et al.* (1962). *The Sources of Invention*. London, Macmillan
   See Chapters 5–7. A classic set of case studies on industrial invention and innovation, and a persuasive attack on the cults of bigness and planning
3. Freeman, C. (1974). *The Economics of Industrial Innovation*. London, Penguin

The most comprehensive synthesis of what we know, and do not know, about industrial innovation.

4. Rosenberg, N. (1976). *Perspectives on Technology.* Cambridge, Cambridge University Press
   Draws heavily on historical studies in order to criticize bland assumptions in economic theory about the nature and dynamics of technological change

RELATED

Technology and economic growth

5. Mansfield, E. *et al.* (1972). 'The Contribution of R & D to Economic Growth in the United States.' *Science,* **175**, 477–486
   Useful review of the economic literature on the relationship between R & D expenditures and economic growth

6. Mansfield, E. (1969). *The Economics of Technological Change.* Harlow, Longmans
   Standard 'text-book' on R & D studies; see especially Chapter 3 'Industrial R & D'

7. Morphet, C. and Green, K. (1977). *Research and Technology as Economic Activities.* London, Butterworths
   Very good introduction to important concepts

8. Rosenberg, N. (1974). *The Economics of Technological Change: Selected Readings.* London, Penguin
   Very useful set of readings, especially Parts 1 and 2

9. Williams, B. (1967). *Investment, Technology and Growth.* London, Chapman & Hall
   A series of essays on the inter-relationships between R & D and economic growth. Thorough but now slightly dated.

Firm size and industrial innovation

10. Baran, P. and Sweezy, P. (1968). *Monopoly Capital.* London, Penguin
    Marxist critique of contemporary capitalism; see especially Chapters 1–3 and pp. 97–110 for discussion of technical innovation

11. Kamien and Schwartz (1975). 'Market Structure and Innovation: A Survey'. *Journal of Economic Literature,* **13**, March, pp. 1–44
    A recent and comprehensive view of evidence on the relationship between innovation and industrial structure

12. Mansfield, E. (1972). *Research and Innovation in the Modern Corporation.* London, Macmillan
    See Chapters 1 and 8

13. Shimshoni, D. (1970). 'The Mobile Scientist in the American Instrument Industry'. *Minerva,* **VIII**, 59–89
    Argues that mobility and 'person-embodied' knowledge are very important in technology transfer. Sees mobile entrepreneurial

scientists important to the continuing important role of small firms in technical innovation. See also Refs. 4, 5 and 17

Planning
14. Burns, T. and Stalker, G. (1961). *The Management of Innovation.* London, Tavistock
    Discussion of organization structures with regard to those that promote innovation; sees 'organic' systems rather than 'mechanistic systems' favoring innovation
15. Norris, K. (1971). 'The Accuracy of Project Cost and Duration Estimates in Industrial R & D'. *R & D Management,* **2**, No. 1
    Present empirical evidence which shows that industrial managers are bad at predicting the cost and outcome of their R & D projects. See also Refs. 4, 5 and 17

Other empirical studies on industrial innovation
16. von Hippel, E. (1976). 'The Dominant Role of Users in the Scientific Instruments Innovation Process'. *Research Policy,* **5**, No. 3, 212–329
    Shows the critically important role of users of scientific instruments in innovation
17. Myers and Marquis, D. (1969). *Successful Industrial Innovations.* Washington, National Science Foundation
    Detailed study of the nature and origins of 567 innovations
18. Science Policy Research Unit (1972). *Success and Failure in Industrial Innovation.* Center for the Study of Industrial Innovation
    A series of studies on paired 'success'–'failure' innovations in scientific instruments and chemical industries. Found that meeting customer needs was most important factor in success
19. OECD (1971). *The Conditions for Success in Industrial Innovations.* Paris, OECD
    Reviews findings of innovation studies published through 1971, by K. Pavitt and S. Wald
20. Rothwell, R. (1976). *Innovation in Textile Machinery.* Occasional Paper No. 2, Science Policy Research Unit, University of Sussex
    Shows that, since the Second World War, technological changes has (a) speeded up, (b) become more radical, (c) originated more and more in R & D laboratories, (d) drawn on a wider spectrum of scientific knowledge and technique, (e) left British and American textile machinery makers behind

The pharmaceutical industry and innovation
21. Cooper, M.H. (1967). *Prices and Profits in the Pharmaceutical Industry.* London, Office of Health Economics
22. Labour Party (1973). *Opposition Green Paper on the Pharmaceutical Industry.* London, Transport House

23. Norton, A. (1973). *Drugs, Science and Society*. London, Fontana
24. Sjostrom, H. and Nilsson, R. (1972). *Thalidomide and the Power of the Drug Companies*. London, Penguin
25. Tealing-Smith, G. (Ed.) (1969). *Economics and Innovation in the Pharmaceutical Industry*. London, Office of Health Economics
    Papers from a symposium held 1967–68. See also Refs. 5 and 12
26. Klass, A. (1975). *There's Gold in Them Thar Pills*. London, Penguin
    A critical look at the pharmaceutical industry

Questions

What are the advantages of large firms and small firms in technical innovation? List these with any reservations and comparative remarks you feel necessary. (See Refs. 1–3, 11, 12, 19.)

What does the empirical evidence tell us about industry's ability to predict and control the expenditures necessary for technical innovation and the buying decisions of eventual customers? (See Refs. 1–3, 15, 19, 25.)

Points for discussion or essays

Describe and discuss the views of Jewkes and Galbraith on the influence of firm size on the volume and effectiveness of industrial R & D and technical innovation. Does the paper on the personal mobility of scientists by Shimshoni satisfactorily resolve the conflicting positions? (See Refs. 1–3, 6, 11, 13, 14, 16.)

'The firm must be large enough to carry large capital commitments of modern technology. It must also be large enough to control its markets' (J.K. Galbraith). Comment. (See Refs. 1, 3, 10–13, 15, 25.)

Discuss the relative importance of 'technology-push' and 'demand-pull' in the process of technical innovation. (See Refs. 3, 4, 8, 13, 16, 19, 20.)

Discuss the notion of 'laissez-innover' in relation to technical innovation in modern industrial society. (See Refs. 1–3, 10, 20, 24.)

It is being increasingly argued that the products of modern industry rather than fulfilling real needs, do in fact create false needs. The drugs industry has received more criticism than most along these lines. The criticisms are well known and include: over-pricing through the effective monopolies given by patents; insufficient testing; advertizing and promotions aimed at medical practitioners; commercial exploitation of ill-health; research for profit not health; the creation of new 'complaints'. Many of these issues crystallize around the issue of safety and demands for stricter regulations. What does the pharmaceutical industry say would be the implications of more stringent drug safety regulations? Are these points justified? What answers to the problems raised can you suggest? (See Refs. 3, 21—26.)

Chapter Five
Government Support of Science and Technology

According to Galbraith's view of the modern industrial state the 'imperatives of technology' have three important consequences: large firms, market planning and government support of science and technology. In the previous Chapter we discussed the first two of these consequences; in this Chapter we shall look at the third. Galbraith's view of government support for science and technology is summed up in the following extract.

> When investment in technological development is very high, a wrong technical judgement or a failure in persuading consumers to buy the product can be extremely expensive. The cost and associated risk can be greatly reduced if the state pays for more exalted technical development or guarantees a market for the technically advanced product. Suitable justification — national defense, national prestige, deeply felt public need, such as for supersonic travel — can readily be found. Modern technology thus defines a growing function of the modern state.

The central question for this topic is, therefore, to what extent do 'technological imperatives' determine government involvement in science and technology in modern industrial nations?

Government support of industrial R & D

The obvious point at which to begin to try to answer this question is the distribution of government expenditures on industrial research and development. (See the Appendix on science and technology statistics.) International comparisons show that there is no clear pattern (*Table 3*). In 1963 in the USA, 57% of industrial R & D was financed by government, whereas in 1964 in the Netherlands only 1% of industrial R & D was government financed. Similarly, in 1969 the equivalent figures for the USA and Japan were 46% and 1%. One might, of course, argue that government involvement in industrial R & D simply reflects the higher level of technological sophistication of US industry. However, if one takes industry-financed R & D as a percentage of Gross National Product as a measure of the technological sophistication of a country's industry, then this is not the case. For example, Dutch industry is technologically sophisticated in this sense, whereas French industry is less sophisticated, but none-theless has a much higher level of government support.

Similarly, if there are 'imperatives of modern technology', they do not appear to be leading to an increase in government support of industrial R & D in all countries. USA government support in this field decreased sharply between 1963 and 1971, and there was a similar trend in Britain.

Finally, inter-industry comparisons of government supported industrial R & D show enormous variation (*Table 4*). It is very high in certain industries and very low in others. In most countries, the aircraft and electrical industries receive substantial government support for their R & D, whereas the chemical and metal industries, often equally sophisticated or large scale, receive very little government assistance. All this evidence suggests that if there are 'imperatives of technology' in government support of R & D, they are by no means universal across industry, across country, or across time.

R & D statistics also show that, in the main, government R & D spending is not related directly to economic growth, but rather to military and other strategic policies (*Table 5*). In the USA the pattern of R & D spending was related to a specific historical period — the Cold War, missile technology, space race, etc. The recent decline in military related R & D does not result from the exhaustion of the possibilities of military and space technology, but from changing economic and political conditions. Similarly, in Britain, the cost of expensive defense and aerospace technology has been increasingly regarded as too heavy for the economy to bear.

Government R & D spending in France, Germany and Britain during the 1960s showed an increasing commitment to civilian projects in aircraft, space, nuclear energy and computers. Again the question can be asked: has this been due to the 'imperatives of technology'? Or something else? In order to try to answer these questions we must first look at the nature of economic and industrial competition in high technology and also the role of government in financing science and technology in a mixed economy.

Technology and the international economy

The most crucial points are that competition in most technologically advanced industry is international in scope and that international flows of science and technology are important for economic growth. The most important single source of industrial technology in the 1960s was the USA, and during that decade, Western Europe imported US technology in ever larger amounts. This was essential for Europe's continued economic growth, but politically it raised the spectre of foreign (i.e. US) economic and political domination. The key to the international flow of US technology to Western Europe became the multinational corporation. As the name suggests, these are companies with manufacturing operations spread through many countries, although top management and R & D activities tend to be concentrated in the 'parent' country. They were seen in Europe as the cause of the migration of qualified manpower to the USA, and as a threat to national sovereignty and autonomous decision making. It was also considered important that rich countries in Western Europe should be competitive in international markets in high technology industries.

However, it was illusory to think that any of the Western European countries, none of which were responsible for more than 10% of the world's science and technology, could hope to be completely self-sufficient in developing all the new technology that it needed. Clearly each of the countries had to specialize and concentrate on its strong points within the world system of science and technology. However, some Western European countries were concerned about becoming completely dependent on the USA for strategically important technologies, both for weapons and for the working of the modern industrial systems.

In some sectors, particularly aircraft, computers, transistors, nuclear energy and scientific instruments, the US technological invasion of Western Europe was linked to spin-offs from the huge American defense and space programs. Thus it induced government financing of civilian R & D projects in the same sectors in Western Europe. When the US technological invasion occurred, European firms and governments (especially De Gaulle in France and Wilson in Britain) were particularly concerned about defense, independence, 'the white-hot technological revolution', prestige, employment and economic competitiveness. The 'technology gap' became almost as serious as the balance of payments deficit. Against this background European governments, often cooperatively or in partnership with large firms, framed a response and developed their own R & D programs.

However, these programs have on the whole been unsuccessful. The original British and French nuclear energy programs have been abandoned. The Concorde is a technical success, but a commercial failure. In European space cooperation, the ELDO rocket never once worked properly and has been abandoned. Advances in solid-state technology and computers have proved expensive, given the US lead. The story of Rolls Royce and the RB211 aircraft engine indicates the scale of the technical and financial gambles that were taken.

The lessons from these experiences do not seem to have been learnt, since there are still large government commitments to high technology industries. The sectional interests of big business, scientists and engineers, trade unions and related government departments are still important, as are the pressures of international economic and political competition. In particular, since the 1973 oil crisis there has been a considerable increase in pressure on governments to finance a more rapid development of nuclear energy technology.

However, despite these failures, Western Europe's industrial R & D improved in strength compared with the USA in other sectors: for example, chemicals, machinery, pharmaceuticals, electrical machinery; the notable exception in this has been Britain.

Government support of science and technology

All government support for science and technology cannot be completely explained through strategic economic considerations. In order to understand more fully government support of industrial R & D we must consider this in the context of overall government support of science and technology. The percentage of total R & D supported by government varies from country to country; in 1969 in France the government—industry ratio was 62—33%, whereas in Japan in the same year it was 14—68%*.

Despite these wide variations a number of features are common. Governments fund R & D activities in areas not covered by private or market initiative; that is, in: (i) fundamental research; (ii) non-market sectors, e.g. defense, health; (iii) sectors where private costs do not fully reflect social costs, e.g. pollution; (iv) agriculture; and (v) industrial technology.

FUNDAMENTAL RESEARCH

We have discussed the economic, political, historical and scientific importance of government support of fundamental research in Chapter 2. In contemporary science policy four main arguments are advanced for government support. These are that (1) fundamental research has uncertain outcomes; (2) it is uncertain where outcomes will be useful; (3) there is often a long time-lag between fundamental discoveries and their application; and (4) it forms an essential part of higher education. Private firms, because of the uncertainties, tend to support fundamental research to an extent below that which is optimal for long-term benefits; hence the importance of government support.

NON-MARKET SECTORS

In modern mixed economies many basic services are not provided by

*For these and the ratios for other countries, see Appendix, *Table 2*

private firms through the market mechanism, but are provided to society as a whole by government. Examples of such services are health, transportation and, of course, defense. As well as providing these services, government also funds the R & D that it thinks is necessary for their provision.

DIVERGENCES BETWEEN SOCIAL AND PRIVATE COSTS

There are also areas of economic activity where the market mechanism creates external costs which it does not meet, and which have to be dealt with through government action. Pollution is a contemporary example, where governments fund the R & D needed for the detection, measurement and reduction of pollution.

AGRICULTURE

Government support of agricultural R & D is in large measure determined by the structure of the industry, where there are a large number of small producers, producing a relatively small range of products, but none of which can afford to perform R & D on an appreciable scale. In many ways, it has been the most successful and indeed socially important part of government R & D, especially in the USA. In its modern form agricultural R & D involves: pure and applied research, technical extension services, education, developmental testing of new agricultural technologies and products themselves. The results and facilities of these services have been made available from agricultural research stations and government technical assistance services to all farmers and producers willing to apply them.

INDUSTRIAL TECHNOLOGY

This is where we rejoin our main concern with industrial technology and consider two challenges to Galbraith's notions of 'imperatives of technology' in terms of government policy for science and technology. These attacks come from Jewkes in Britain and from Eads and Nelson in the USA. Both argue that, when industry thinks the risks and economic returns are right, it will invest its own money in big and expensive technology. For example, the Boeing Company and the 747 Jumbo Jet, and IBM and the 360 series of computers. Furthermore, they point out, in spite of growing scale, industry in general has been spending more of its own money on R & D over the past 70 years. From this they argue that governments will inevitably be asked to finance only 'second best' projects, or the more speculative and difficult R & D. In such circumstances it is very difficult for governments to stop projects that are likely to be unsuccessful, given the action of political lobbies, sectional interests and pressure groups. Indeed, it may even be difficult for governments to recognize that a project is going to be unsuccessful, from their lack of knowledge of market considerations governing the scale of the resulting product (e.g. Concorde).

These factors lead Jewkes, Eads and Nelson to propose a different role for government in industrial R & D that avoids taking on 'second best' projects and the 'throwing of good money after bad'. They argue that government-supported industrial R & D should be used to improve the basic 'state of the art' in technology through pilot and demonstration projects, rather than to replace industry in financing full-scale commercial development. Their model is similar to the role of government R & D in agriculture described above.

These arguments suggest that the 'imperatives of technology' have not been the main reasons for government support of industrial R & D; rather, strategic, economic and political factors have been the most important. This may well be the case to date, but it is possible to argue that Galbraith was only slightly premature in his analysis and that technologies are only *now* beginning to assert their own scale imperative. The obvious example is nuclear power where, in Europe at least, the costs, risks, scale, complexity, etc., do seem to derive from technological considerations; other examples might include faster trains, offshore oil recovery and other energy technologies. These examples, in looking to the future, raise an important question and one which forms the basis for the seminar in this topic. The question is: What sorts of R & D should governments be funding? Associated with this are the problems of how, where and by whom should it be performed?

Reading

ESSENTIAL

1. Galbraith, J.K. (1967). *The New Industrial State.* London, Penguin (1974)
   Scale imperatives of technology and government involvement
2. Freeman, C. (1974). *The Economics of Industrial Innovation.* London, Penguin
   See Part 3. Suggestions for new directions for government policy
3. Freeman, C. *et al.* (1971). 'The Goals of R & D in the 1970s'. *Science Studies,* 1, 357–406
   A strong critique of government policies in the 1960s
4. Nelson, R. (1971). ' "World Leadership" the "Technology Gap" and National Science Policy.' *Minerva,* IX, 386–399
   A sceptical look at government R & D programs justified in terms of an international technological race

49

Science, technology and government
5. OECD (1971). *The Conditions for Success in Technological Innovation.* Paris, OECD
   See Part III. Reviews trends in government funding of R & D
6. Gilpin, R. (1970). 'Technological Strategies and National Purpose.' *Science,* **169,** 441–448
   A thought-provoking discussion of different countries' approaches to technological development
7. Fabian, Y, Young, A. *et al.* (1975). *Changing Priorities for Government R & D.* Paris, OECD
   An excellent reference document, giving detailed trends in government R & D spending between 1961 and 1972, as well as descriptions of government machinery concerned with R & D, in the major OECD countries
8. Fabian, Y., Young, A. *et al.* (1975). *Patterns of Resources Devoted to Research and Experimental Development.* Paris, OECD
   A shorter book than Ref. 7, giving the essential features of R & D spending in the main OECD countries between 1963 and 1971
9. Bernal, J.D. (1939). *The Social Function of Science.* London, Routledge; Cambridge, Mass., MIT Press (1967)
   Classic. See especially Part II 'What Science Could Do'
10. Poole, J.B. and Andrews, E.K. (1973). *The Government of Science in Britain.* London, Weidenfeld and Nicolson
    A selection of readings on British science policy. See especially Introductory essay and readings in Chapters 3 and 4
11. Price, D.K. (1953). *Government and Science.* Oxford, Oxford University Press (1962)
    Discusses the development of relations between science and government in post-war America; especially concerned with freedom of scientific enterprise.
12. (1971). *A Framework for Government R & D.* Green Paper, Cmnd 4814. London, HMSO. White Paper, Cmnd 5046. London, HMSO (1972)
    The Rothschild Report and subsequent White Paper. Supposedly established the legitimacy of the 'customer/contractor' principle. For commentary on the debate that it engendered see *New Scientist,* December 71–April 72, especially edition dated 2 December 1971

Government support of industrial R & D
13. Nelson, R. (1971). 'The Simple Economics of Basic Scientific Research.' In *The Economics of Technological Change.* Ed. N. Rosenberg. London, Penguin
    Classic economic justification of government support for basic research

14. OECD (1966). *Governments and Technical Innovation.* Paris, OECD
    Notes increasing government involvement (NB 1964–66) in tech-
    nical innovation in certain sectors. Sees this as due to costs, risks
    and inadequacy of market in certain areas. Warns of problems of
    cost and public control
15. Nelson, R., Peck, M.J. and Kalachek, E.D. (1967). *Technology,
    Economic Growth and Public Policy.* Washington, The Brookings
    Institution
    See Part III. Argues R & D 'should be viewed as one among a
    wider range of public policy instruments' and integrated with
    general policy measures and objectives. Important book
16. Eads, G. and Nelson, R.R. (1971). 'Governmental Support of
    Advanced Civilian Technology: Power Reactors and the Supersonic
    Transport.' *Public Policy*, XIX, No. 3, 405–428
    Argues against trend for governments to fund big technology
    projects on grounds of cost and public control. Proposes a dif-
    ferent role for government in financing industrial R & D which
    improves 'the state of the art'.
17. Eads, G. (1974). 'US Government Support for Civilian Tech-
    nology: Economic Theory versus Political Practice.' *Research
    Policy*, 3, 2–16
    Discussion of a major gap between the economic concept of
    externalities as a justification for US Government intervention in
    the process of developing commercial technology, and the
    direction that this intervention appears to be taking. Unless the
    economic profession provides an operational concept of externali-
    ties for use by decision makers, externalities may be discovered
    primarily whenever it is politically advantageous to do so
18. Jewkes, J. (1972). *Government and High Technology.* Occasional
    Paper No. 57. London, Institute for Economic Affairs
    Argues brilliantly against government support of big technology
    from a non-interventionist, *laissez-faire* position
19. Gibbons, M. and Johnston, R. (1974). 'The Roles of Science in
    Technological Innovation.' *Research Policy*, 3, No. 3, 220–244
    Important empirical study showing the significance of scientific
    information and knowledge as background for technological
    problem-solvers in industry
20. Pavitt, K. and Walker, W. (1976). 'Government Policies towards
    Industrial Innovation: A Review.' *Research Policy*, 5, No. 1, 11–97
    A thorough review of the literature. Includes information on
    government policies in France, West Germany, Netherlands and
    the UK
21. Pavitt, K. 'Government Policies towards Industrial Innovation: A
    Review of Empirical Findings.' *Omega*, to be published
    Argues that most OECD governments are misallocating resources
    to industrial R & D

International aspects of technology

22. OECD (1970). *Gaps in Technology — Analytical Report.* Book 4. 'International Economic Exchanges', 237–300. Paris, OECD
   Shows Western countries are moving towards increasing inter-dependence in technological capabilities; role of US companies particularly important in innovation and diffusion
23. Pavitt, K. (1973). 'Technology, International Competition and Economic Growth: Some Lessons and Perspectives.' *World Politics,* **XXV**, No. 2, 188–205
   Shows that over the 1960s as a whole the USA lost much of its technological leadership and that small and medium-sized nations have evolved viable policies for industrial technology
24. Vernon, R. (Ed.) (1970). *The Technology in International Trade.* New York, Columbia University Press
   An attempt to integrate technology as an explicit variable in the economic theories of international trade

Case studies of specific projects or programs

25. Costello, J. and Hughes, T. (1971). *The Battle for Concorde.* London, Compton Press
   Discusses the project in terms of management of advanced technology and its survival through strong political opposition. Implicitly supports Concorde
26. Wilson, A. (1973). *The Concorde Fiasco.* London, Penguin
   Discusses both the political and technical aspects of the project and argues for its immediate cancellation
27. Gray, R. (1971). *Rolls on the Rocks.* London, Compton Press and Panther
   A history of Rolls Royce. Part 3 contains details of RB 211 and collapse. Book lacks analysis
28. Hamilton, D. (1971). 'Advanced Passenger Train Revealed.' *New Scientist,* **50**, 624–625
   Describes development of project
29. Atomic Energy Authority (1976). *Energy R & D in the UK.* Harwell, UKAEA
   An apparently sophisticated attempt to identify priority areas for energy R & D in the UK, which ends up giving the highest priority to the fast breeder reactor
30. Surrey, A.J., Chesshire, J. and Dombey, N. (1976). 'The hazards of rushing to build a nuclear fast reactor.' *The Times,* 28 June
   A criticism of the assumptions underlying Ref. 29
31. *Annual Reports on US Energy Outlook.* Washington, Federal Energy Administration
   Contain forecasts of future trends, many of which are of questionable validity
32. (1976). *A National Plan for Energy Research, Development and*

Demonstration: Creating Energy Choices for the Future. Washington, Energy Research and Development Administration
33. Rand Corporation (1976). *Analysis of Federally Funded Demonstration Projects.* Washington, US Department of Commerce
Analyses the experience of the US Government in supporting industrial innovation
34. Arthur D. Little Inc. (1976). *Federal Funding of Civilian Research and Development.* Washington, US Department of Commerce
Same as Ref. 33

Questions

How do Galbraith's views on the increasing government involvement with industrial R & D compare with the empirical evidence of science and technology statistics? (See Refs. 1–3, 7, 8, Appendix.)

What case can be made for government involvement in industrial technology in a mixed economy? Should governments give financial support for specific commercial development ventures in industry? If so, why? If not, why not? What is your view of the British experience in this field with projects like the Rolls Royce RB 211 and Concorde? (See Refs. 1–3, 5, 6, 12, 16, 21, 25, 26.)

Points for discussion or essays

Describe and discuss the reasons given for government support of science and technology in modern industrial society. Comment upon the importance of these various reasons in the formulation and implementation of government policy for science and technology. (See Refs. 1–5, 7, 10–12, 18.)

'When investment in technological development is very high, a wrong technical judgement or a failure in persuading consumers to buy can be extremely expensive. The cost and associated risk can be greatly reduced if the state pays for more exalted technical development or guarantees a market for the technically advanced product' (Galbraith). Discuss this viewpoint with reference to one or more of the following high technology projects:
   supersonic transport and Concorde
   nuclear power reactors
   government-financed demonstration projects in the USA
(See Refs. 1, 4, 16–18, 25–34.)

Chapter Six
Science and Technology in the United States of America

Many discussions of modern industrial society take as their model the USA. In our discussions of modern industrial society, we also took the USA as our exemplar, and looked in some detail at the inter-relationships between science, technology, the military, industry and government. In this chapter we want to go beyond this material, paying particular attention to the American institutions and experi-ence, and to some more recent changes. Our main question for this topic is: in what ways has the US responded to the problems of modern science and technology?

From the end of the Second World War until the mid-1960s there was a prolonged 'honeymoon' in the USA between scientists, science and technology on the one hand, and the Government, industry and public on the other. There was a massive growth in the resources devoted to science and technology. Federal R & D expenditure rose from approximately $74 million in 1940 to $12.2 billion in 1962–63, and to $16.5 billion in 1967–68, a growth rate of about 12% per annum at current prices.

The Federal Government's policies for science and technology have been mediated in two ways; firstly, by the creation of 'operating agencies' and, secondly, by the use and placing of 'contracts' with private firms. The most important agencies for Federal R & D have been: the National Science Foundation (NSF), Atomic Energy Commission (AEC), National Aeronautics and Space Administration (NASA), Department of Health, Education and Welfare (HEW) and, of course, The Department of Defense (DOD). Although all of these have been subject to changes in public policy and priorities, they have nonetheless become politically powerful and at times difficult to control. The only agency not to become power-ful has been the NSF, which is concerned mainly with basic research. These agencies have 'contracted out' R & D and production to private industry, which has further exacerbated problems of public control, especially by blurring the distinction between 'public' and 'private' sectors. Thus, though the Federal Government is the major source of funds for R & D, private industry is the main performer (see Appendix).

This massive commitment of resources to science and technology was made in response to four factors. Firstly, the post-war emergence of the US as the major world political power, and the subsequent Cold War with the USSR. Secondly, the technological predominance of US industry in the post-war period, stemming from the supremacy developed during and immediately after the Second World War. Thirdly, and resulting from the first two points, a desire for overall US pre-eminence in science and technology in terms of facilities, manpower, important breakthroughs, technological capabilities, etc. Finally, a tremendous optimism on the part of scientists and the public that science and technology could and would solve all the world's problems.

Science in modern America

Since the mid 1960s, however, there has been a fundamental change. US predominance in both civil and military science and technology has been challenged. In the military field, increased costs, decreasing security and Russian military advances have led to attempts by both the USA and USSR to reach some agreement on the stabilization of the arms race. In civilian technology, the US lead has been successfully challenged by Japan and West Germany, to the extent that America had a substantial trade deficit by the end of the 1960s, and in 1971 had to devalue the dollar.

There has also emerged a general disenchantment with science and technology. Some, like Roszak, have gone so far as to see it as a general rejection of the scientific outlook and a move towards a more mystical view of nature. This questioning of science and technology as being necessarily progressive and beneficial has been in response to a number of factors. Particularly important have been the uses made of science and technology in South East Asia, environmental problems, and the emergent futility of putting men on the Moon. So influential had this disenchantment become, that in 1971 the leading figure in American Science policy, Harvey Brooks, wrote a defensive article in *Science* entitled 'Can Science Survive in the Modern Age'. Clearly the honeymoon was over.

A second major change has been in the type and degree of the Federal Government's commitment to university research, with the latter becoming less dependent on military and space agencies for research grants. Various moves to completely cut out military funding of university research have had a cumulative impact in scaling down the reliance of universities on the military. Pressures from students and university academics themselves have accelerated moves in this direction. Funds available for university research have, as a consequence, levelled off. This has created certain problems, but has meant that research projects can no longer be justified purely on the grounds that 'the Russians are doing it'. Slowly and painfully it has been realized that the US cannot be 'second to none' in all areas of science and technology. The fact that other countries were able to import and utilize the results of US R & D made the point that the US could import science and technology from countries such as Japan, Western Europe and the USSR.

Thirdly, there has been a growing debate about the nature and policy implications of this scientific, technological and industrial challenge. Some argue that it is simply that other countries have caught up after the disruption and dislocation of World War II; now that the USA no longer tries to maintain unrealistic exchange rates against other countries, there is no reason why US industry should fall behind in technology and growth. Other observers argue that the problems are deeper. The USA will eventually fall behind in industrial technology, if US firms continue to be able to find easy profits through overseas investment, and if large-scale defense and space programs continue to drain high quality scientists and engineers out of economically more important industrial sectors, like iron and steel, and machine tools.

Although many observers have tended to agree with the latter set of arguments, there has been less agreement about what the US Federal Government can or should do about it. Aerospace firms have tried to turn what is perhaps a genuine general problem to their own sectoral advantage. In the late 1960s and early 1970s they obtained Federal money for civilian projects, such as the supersonic transport and novel methods of urban transportation. The former was cancelled through a vote by the US Congress in 1971, and the latter led to technologically sophisticated contraptions, which often did not work, and were replaced by conventional buses, trams, trolleys and trains. After the 1973 oil embargo, however, the Energy Research and Development Commission (ERDA) has replaced the old Atomic Energy Commission, with a much-expanded government program of energy R & D. Whilst most observers agree that such a program is necessary, ERDA's programs have been criticized for the low priority given to energy conservation, the high priority given to nuclear energy, and the danger of giving money to industrial firms to do R & D which they would have done anyway with their own money.

The final important change has been that scientists and technologists have increasingly turned their attention directly towards 'social problems', arguing that they can help with their solution. Clearly, in the face of reduced expenditures and growing public hostility, scientists have attempted to make their science more 'relevant'. Examples of the kind of 'social problems' canvassed by scientists and technologists as suitable for their attention are: environmental pollution and despoliation, urban and housing conditions, drug addiction, overpopulation, and even the problem of racial minorities. A leading proponent of this view has been the leading nuclear physicist and senior scientific statesman Alvin Weinberg, who in 1966 asked

Can we identify Quick Technological Fixes for profound and almost infinitely complicated social problems, 'fixes' that are within the grasp of modern technology and which would either eliminate the social problem without requiring a change in the individual's social attitudes, or would so alter the problem as to make its resolution more feasible?

More recently, Weinberg has been a leading advocate of 'technology assessment', another related attempt to make science and technology more socially relevant.

(Technology Assessment is) a systematic, comprehensive, objective value-free analysis of the consequences of technological applications for society.

The underlying hope of both 'technological fixes' and 'technology assessment' is that just as technical problems can be 'solved' by scientific technology per se, so social problems can be 'solved' by the application of science and technology.

In the reading and seminar discussions we would like you to explore either one or both of the following topics. Firstly, the changes in US R & D in the past ten years, particularly the reasons underlying these changes and their consequences. Secondly, the notions of 'technological fixes' and 'technology assessment', particularly the assumptions they make about 'social problems' and their solutions.

Reading

ESSENTIAL

1. Gilpin, R. (1975). *Technology, Economic Growth and International Competitiveness*. Paper prepared for the Subcommittee on Economic Growth of the Joint Economic Committee, US Congress, Washington, 9 July
   Traces the relative technological decline of the USA, warns of the dangers of 'post-imperial' inefficiency like that of UK industry, and proposes a policy of technological rejuvenation
2. Lakoff, S. (1973). 'The Vicissitudes of American Science Policy at Home and Abroad.' *Minerva*, **XI**, 175—190
   The problems of US science policy in the early 1970s
3. Etzioni, A. and Remp, R. (1972). 'Technological "Shortcuts" to Social Change.' *Science*, **175**, 31—38
   How technology can help solve US social problems (?)

4. Wynne, B. (1973). 'Technology Assessment — superfix or super-
fixation.' *Science for People*, No. 24, Nov.—Dec.
Effective criticism of the technology fix/technology assessment
movement

FURTHER

Historical background
5. Daniels, G. (1967). 'The Process of Professionalisation of American
Science.' *Isis*, **58**, 151—166
Discusses the justifications for, and problems of, the emerging
professional activity of science in the period 1820—60
6. Dupree, H.A. (1957). *Science in the Federal Government*.
Cambridge, Mass., Harvard University Press
The only comprehensive account of American science policy and
science institutions in the period to 1940, until the bicentennial
literature explosion of 1976
7. Greenberg, D. (1970). *The Politics of American Science*. London,
Penguin
See Chapters 3 and 12. An incisive and irreverent account of
government/science relations in the USA
8. Rosenberg, N. (1976). *The Role of Science and Technology in
American National Development*. Published by the US National
Academy of Sciences as part of the Bicentennial celebration.
Stanford, Stanford University Press
An excellent account of how the USA grew out of technological
dependence after economic independence
9. Van Tassel, D.D. and Hall, M.G. (Eds.) (1966). *Science and
Society in the United States*. Homewood, Illinois, Dorsey Press
A series of essays on the place and role of science in various aspects
of American society in the period to 1960. Most essays are, how-
ever, on the nineteenth century and earlier. Most are very good

Science and government
10. OECD (1968). *Reviews of National Science Policy: USA*. Paris,
OECD
Encyclopaedic and thorough, discusses major institutions, but
surprisingly has little to say on massive defense R & D
11. Price, D.K. (1954). *Science and Government*. Oxford, Oxford
University Press (1962)
Pioneering study of the special problems that science poses for
government. See especially Chapter 11 'Freedom or Responsibility'
and Chapter 3 'Federation by Contract'
12. Price, D.K. (1968). *The Scientific Estate*. Cambridge, Mass.,
Harvard University Press
Not as good as his earlier book and in many ways more dated.

Discusses the growing influence of scientists in public policy in the USA

13. Beckler, D. (1974). 'The Precarious Life of Science in the White House.' *Daedalus*, Summer, 115–134
   An insider's account of the role of science in the White House in the 1960s

14. Smith, B.L. (1973). 'A New Science Policy in the United States'. *Minerva*, **XI**, 162–174
   Discusses recent changes in US science policy; reflects interest in changing priorities

Technology and US economic competitiveness

15. Boffey, P. (1971). 'Technology and World Trade: Is There Cause for Alarm.' *Science*, **172**, 37–41
   Discusses concern over possible loss of American predominance in 'technology intensive' industries. Notes disagreement amongst economists over this loss and over whether it is a serious matter

16. Brooks, H. (1972). 'What's Happening to the US Lead in Technology.' *Harvard Business Review*, May/June, 100–118
   Argues that US lead has been lost because of post-war 'catching-up' by Western Europe and Japan, and because of disillusionment with growth at higher levels of income

17. Boretsky, M. (1975). 'Trends in US Technology: A Political Economist's View.' *American Scientist*, January/February
   Argues that the USA has already lost its technological lead in many sectors, and that US multinational firms harm the USA by exporting technology to other countries

18. Gilpin, R. (1975). *US Power and the Multinational Corporation.* London, Macmillan
   Puts forward the unfashionable argument that US multinational firms are not in the American self-interest, since they enable cheap and easy profits abroad, instead of industrial regeneration at home

19. National Science Board. *Science Indicators.* (annually). Regular publications on trends in R & D expenditures in government and industry. Washington, National Science Foundation
   Essential and excellent statistical information, necessary for monitoring policy trends. In particular: is industry-financed R & D increasing in real terms? What is happening to government-financed energy R & D? Is military R & D on the increase again?

20. McGraw Hill Publications (1976). 'Where Private Industry puts its Research Money.' *Business Week*, 28 June, 62–84
   Excellent survey of R & D expenditures by big US companies, and of technological trends in different industries

'Anti-science' in the US

21. Beckwith, J. (1971). 'The Scientists in Opposition in the United

States.' In *The Social Impact of Modern Biology*. Ed. W. Fuller. London, Routledge Kegan Paul

Discusses the role of the 'radical' scientist in relation to the problems facing modern science, particularly the biologists in American society

22. Brooks, H. (1971). 'Can Science Survive in the Modern Age?' *Science*, **174**, 21—30

Discusses, from the point of view of policy, reactions against science. Argues that science is being misused, but can still respond to new social priorities

23. Reich, C.A. (1972). *The Greening of America*. London, Penguin

Very influential and much criticized book in the USA; tries to assess the long-term impact of the major social changes of the 1960s, especially the peace and youth movements

24. Roszak, T. (1970). *The Making of a Counter Culture*. London, Faber

Account of 'hippie-protest' movement, especially their rejection of science and technology

'Technology' and social problems

25. Freeman, C. (1971). 'Technology Assessment in its Social Context.' *Studium Generale*, **24**, 1038—1050

Reviews the potential of technology assessment as an aid to public decision making in science and technology

26. Hetman, F. (1973). *Society and the assessment of technology: premises, concepts, methodology, experiments, areas of application*. Paris, OECD

Systematic account of methods of technology assessment, written largely by their proponents

27. Strasser, G. (1972) 'Technology Assessment A Fad or a New Way of Life?' *Science Policy Reviews*, **5**, (1), 7—13

Shows the links between technology assessment (TA), the systems approach and technological fixes. Sees TA as an essential element in the 'evolutionary overhaul' of our 'system'

28. Weinberg, A. (1966). 'Can Technology Replace Social Engineering.' *Science and Public Affairs (Bull. At. Sci.)*, **22**, (2), 4—8

Assumes all social change requires social engineering. Argues that social engineering has been unsuccessful; therefore we need something that will work, namely, technology

29. Wynne, B. (1973). 'The Rhetoric of Consensus Politics: a Critical Review of Technology Assessment.' *Research Policy*, **4**, No. 2, 108—158

Critique of TA. Reveals TAs naive view of politics and the political process, and its limited view of the social context of technology

30. Etzioni, A. and Remp, R. (1973). *Technological Shortcuts to*

Social Change. New York, Russell Sage Foundation
Extended version of Ref. 4
31. Simmons, H. (1973). 'Systems Dynamics and Technocracy.' In *Thinking About the Future: A Critique of 'The Limits to Growth'.* Ed. H.S.D. Cole *et al.* London, Chatto and Windus
Reveals the political values underlying the apparently value-free method of 'systems dynamics'. Suggests that the technocratic tradition has deep roots in the USA

Points for discussion or essays

Discuss the nature and implications of changes in the US world position in industrial technology. In this context, compare and contrast the arguments of Brooks, Boretsky and Gilpin. (See Refs. 1, 15–20.)

Discuss the 'disenchantment' with science in the late 1960s. To what extent was the youth 'counter-culture' representative of all American youth, and all American society? In what way did it influence the allocation of resources to US science and technology? (See Refs. 2, 13, 14, 19, 21–24.)

Discuss the reasons for the changes in US R & D spending since the Second World War. What are likely to be the consequences of the most recent changes? (See Refs. 1, 2, 6, 10, 13, 14, 19, 20.)

'Scientists and engineers are often surprised when they find that problems of urban blight, social unrest, environmental pollution, inadequate education opportunities, and health care deficiencies do not respond neatly to scientific and technological initiatives' (Ref. 27). Discuss. (See Refs. 3, 4, 25, 28, 30.)

'An assessment of the social impact of technology can be nothing but of benefit to mankind.' Discuss. (See Refs. 6, 25–27, 29.)

Chapter Seven
Science and Technology in
Western Europe

Now that Britain has decided to remain in the European Economic Community, relations between Britain and Western Europe in science and technology will remain strong for the foreseeable future. These will be formed through close relations in trade and industry, common external problems like oil supply and commodity prices, and the commitments made to international cooperation in science and technology. It therefore makes sense in discussing science and technology to consider Western European countries together, especially since most of the problems they face are common ones, and there may be a common lesson to be learnt.

There are three main problems Western European countries have had to face with regard to science and technology since the Second World War. First, no European nation is any longer scientifically and technologically preponderant. All countries depend to a great extent on international flows in technology. Countries have had to decide what technologies to import and what to develop themselves, and how to achieve the former through licensing, trade and foreign investment.

The second problem stems from the first: countries have increasingly been faced with the problem of priorities. No country can do everything or lead the field in every sphere; thus they have had to 'specialize'. The decision to specialize, and the determination of what fields to specialize in, has not necessarily been made centrally or even explicitly by countries. Rather it has emerged from an awareness of their own and competitors' strengths and weaknesses.

Thirdly, all countries have had to decide on a policy towards big technology. They have had problems in maintaining viable programs, especially in aircraft, nuclear energy, advanced electronics and space. These have grown out of increasingly large scale, heavy R & D costs, technical and commercial risks, the influence of strategic interests, the interrelationship between the military and civil industry, and the US lead in most of these fields stemming from the 1950s.

The main questions for this chapter are: How have the major Western European countries coped with these common problems? What developments and policies will shape the future of Western European science and technology? To begin to answer the first of these questions we will look at the experience of the three largest countries — Britain, France and West Germany.

Britain

British science, technology, industrial and indeed general policy since 1945 reflects a reluctant but steady retreat from the position of a world-wide imperial power to that of a medium-sized European power. At the end of the Second World War, although having suffered some destruction, British industry was fairly strong in advanced technology. There was a big aircraft industry and an advanced nuclear capability with close technological links with the USA through wartime arrangements and subsequent defense agreements. This, together with worldwide political activities and commitments, made Britain a first-rank world technological power. In the 1950s Britain attempted to continue this role. It developed its own independent nuclear weapons and undertook ambitious programs in civilian nuclear and aircraft technology. At the same time, in the face of manpower shortages in science and technology, spending on science and engineering education increased rapidly.

The election at the end of the 1950s was won on the slogan 'You've never had it so good'. Nevertheless, consumer prosperity masked real problems in Britain's industry. A number of factors emerged which revealed the underlying weakness of the British economy. First, British industry had not been particularly innovative, nor had it really taken advantage of modern technological developments. Second, there was the growing economic status of the rest of Europe, particularly those countries that formed the EEC in 1958. Third, the resource and market base of Britain was very small in comparison with the USA. Fourth, British political commitments diminished with the end of the Empire, whilst the costs of technological development increased with growing scale, complexity and risks.

The 1950s were characterized by a mismatch between political and economic ambition, and economic and technological reality. The result was a series of expensive and costly failures in advanced technology. In civil nuclear technology, the initial euphoria of building the first commercial reactor in 1956 at Calder Hall was not sustained in subsequent development, nor were sufficient reactors sold abroad to offset development costs. In civilian aircraft the British record was equally bad. The Comet, Britannia, Vanguard and VC 10 were commercial failures, the one success of the decade being the turbo-prop Viscount. Later the TSR2 and Concorde continued the sorry story. The saga was more o. less repeated in Britain's abortive rocket program . . . Blue Streak, Black Knight, etc.

In the early 1960s, British R & D expenditures were still rising and the newly established Ministry of Science made the first steps towards trying to establish a policy for science and technology. Science and technology were still an essentially non-party issue and there was little public debate about policy. After 1963 all this changed and science and technology became one of the major issues in the 1964 election. In 1963, with a view to the impending election, the Labour Party sought to be identified as the party of 'change' or in Harold Wilson's phrase 'the White Hot Technological Revolution'. The Labour Party became committed to a platform of 'socialism and science', with the objectives of making British industry more technologically competitive, of spending more on science and technology, of halting the brain-drain, and of developing economic and industrial planning.

The instrument of these policies later became the Ministry of Technology. Despite these apparent changes, the main problems are still unsolved today. The Government remains heavily committed to large-scale government-financed programs of R & D related to defense, civil aviation and nuclear energy. The powerful vested interests remain, protected by growing nationalism, and a cloak of government secrecy greater than in any other supposedly liberal democracy. At the same time, there is the continuing technological backwardness of British industry. In spite of the brave talk of the technological revolution, Britain's relative productivity and world export share in manufactured goods has continued to decline in the 1970s. Industry-financed R & D is much lower than in West Germany and Japan, and engineering goods are of inferior technical quality. School leavers are reluctant to go into science and, even more so, into engineering. Even when they do, they are still reluctant to go to work in industry. After two World Wars and forty years of protected Empire markets, British industry finds itself in the same position as at the beginning of this century: industrially and technically inferior to Germany and the USA, with the difference now that Japan and France will soon join them.

France

France has had the same sad experience as Britain with big technology, but ten years later. Before the Second World War, French industry was weak and protected. After the war, France, unlike Britain, had virtually no advanced technological effort and no special technological links with the USA. However, in the 1950s it did begin a small nuclear program in both military and civil spheres, and the small aircraft industry made cheap, simple and successful military planes, as well as the Caravelle.

This somewhat backward position in science and technology persisted until 1958, but with the coming to power of Charles de Gaulle and the foundation of the 5th Republic, French industrial, technological and scientific policy was given a major stimulus. With de Gaulle came the notions of economic modernization and independence. He saw clearly that science and technology were closely bound up with these objectives. The *Délégation Générale à la Recherche Scientifique et Technique* (DGRST) was set up to provide direct advice to both the Prime Minister and the Interministerial Commission responsible for R & D policy. From this one commentator has said 'On paper France has the most logical and clear-cut machinery for science policy of any major West European country'. However, the important defense, space and nuclear sectors remained outside this machinery and under direct Presidential control.

After the settlement of the Algerian War in the early 1960s, de Gaulle accelerated France's nuclear weapons program and gave it top priority, so that in 1967 France became the fourth thermonuclear power. The associated development of delivery systems through the supersonic Mirage bomber to nuclear-powered missile-firing submarines had spin-offs for both the aerospace industry and satellite technology. The French aircraft industry, though small, had a number of successes, particularly with the Caravelle and the Mirage fighters, but because of the small home market increasingly sought to undertake projects on a cooperative basis, e.g. Concorde and the Airbus. The French independent space program was very modest but did succeed in getting four satellites into orbit. The civil nuclear program developed similar technology to the first generation of British reactors. However, it was some years behind Britain and was never commercially adopted. French initiatives in developing a color television system, and in establishing a French computer industry, while politically attractive in the short-term, have had technical and economic difficulties.

Since de Gaulle's departure in 1969, there has been a steady move away from the ambition of complete technological autarchy in the high technologies. In computers, nuclear energy and aircraft, there has been a greater willingness to buy American technology whilst — like the Japanese — keeping managerial control firmly in French hands. When one looks at the high technologies in 1976, it can be argued that Britain now suffers from greater technological nationalism than the French do.

Britain and France have diverged in two other important respects. First, in spite of heavy national commitments to the high technologies, a continuing industrial dynamism has emerged since the Second World War, transforming France from a backward agricultural country to one of the richest in the world. The general level of industrial R & D and technical quality has been part of this transformation. Second, since the oil embargo in 1973, France's energy situation has been very exposed. Unlike the UK, it does not have abundant coal and (with the North Sea) oil and gas reserves. It has therefore committed itself much more vigorously to nuclear energy. In particular, with the minority participation of West Germany and Italy, France has decided to build a full-scale sodium-cooled fast breeder reactor. The consequences of this decision will be enormous.

West Germany

The West German situation confirms one theme of this topic that no one learns from others' mistakes. Germany's commitment to big technology in the early 1970s is like France's ten years ago and Britain's twenty years ago. After the Second World War Germany's industrial base was shattered and its former status as the scientifically and technologically major country lost. As part of the terms of surrender, its remaining defense industries were dismantled, its patents and overseas assets confiscated, and many of the best scientists and technologists taken to work in either the USA or USSR. Allied restrictions on arms, aircraft and nuclear industries, and the lack of any national science policy, made West Germany seem comparatively backward in science and technology.

In post-war reconstruction, however, essential organizational and technological skills of pre-war Germany remained and were developed. Reconstruction enabled German industry to start from scratch with new technologies. With a small and restricted defense industry, West Germany had no temptation to compete with the US in aircraft, nuclear technology, electronics and space, as Britain and France tried, but did not succeed, in doing. West German government expenditure on R & D remained at a lower percentage of total R & D than in Britain and France (see Appendix, *Table 4*). West Germany concentrated investment and R & D activity in economically important industrial sectors, such as chemicals, mechanical industry and electricals, and where it could not afford the necessary R & D, as in computers and nuclear technology, it bought licenses from the USA. This was the basis of West Germany's post-war industrial resurgence.

In the mid-1960s, however, West Germany, like Japan, began to worry about being an economic giant, but a political dwarf. One solution to this 'problem', that the German government increasingly favored, was to move into big technology programs. Government expenditures in nuclear technology, aircraft, computers and space have increased. These areas were chosen for various reasons: nuclear technology, in order to build on the strength of German industry (Kraftwerkunion); aircraft, owing to the activities of pressure groups; and computers in response to US dominance of the German market in this field. Of these activities, only the nuclear program has been successful; the space program has stabilized, and the aircraft and computer programs have yet to prove themselves. The German economy and German industry remain the strongest in Europe, so the temptation to continue to expand its activities in high technology remains. It is doubtful whether, nuclear energy apart, it will be more successful than France or Britain.

The Lessons

In relation to the objectives of defense, economic growth, economic independence, social welfare and environmental problems, the performance of Western European science and technology has been mixed. West Germany has had phenomenal economic growth, while accepting strategic dependence. France, having made 'independence' its main goal, was successful in developing a nuclear weapons capability, in achieving a rapid rate of economic growth and industrial modernization. The British performance has been less than satisfactory. Economic growth has continued, but at a much slower rate than in the rest of Europe and the independent nuclear deterrent has been retained, but with strong technological dependence on the USA. Industrial independence appears not to have altered significantly since the initial US penetration of the 1950s and early 1960s.

In Western Europe as a whole, social welfare and environmental problems have appeared less serious than in either the USA or Japan. Their experiences suggests that there is no economic advantage and little political prestige to be gained from big technology programs. Most such programs have wasted money and resources, created vested interests that make public control difficult, and have been politically embarassing.

These experiences suggest that government involvement in big technology should be drastically reduced. Against this many argue that, without such government support, scientific and technological activity would dry up. If this were to be the case it would be important and a major justification for government support of big technology. However, countries like Switzerland and the Netherlands have very low government R & D expenditures indeed, yet are by no means scientifically or industrially backward. On the contrary, they have very high levels of industrial and fundamental R & D. They are, however, more specialized than bigger Western European countries; for example, Netherlands in electronics, Switzerland in pharmaceuticals. Both are open to world commercial and scientific competition. Both also have excellent higher education and research facilities, and place great emphasis on teaching foreign languages. All these factors facilitate long-term competitiveness in international markets. The experience of these small West European countries shows that scientific and technological strength is not necessarily dependent upon government commitment to big technology projects.

Attempts at European technological cooperation have been almost exclusively in big technologies. Proponents have argued that the scale imperatives of modern technology make such cooperation — and eventual European integration — inevitable. Sceptics point to the not very impressive achievements over the past twenty years, and argue that political cooperation must precede, rather than follow from, technological cooperation.

Reading

ESSENTIAL

1. Papon, P. (1975). 'The State and Technological Competition in France.' *Research Policy*, **4**, No. 3, 214–244
   A critical analysis of Gaullist policies towards the high technologies
2. Keck, O. (1974). 'West German Science Policy since the early 1960's: trends and objectives.' *Research Policy*, **5**, No. 2, 116–157
   Describes changing German government priorities since the early 1960s. Is sceptical of both official justifications, and radical explanations, of these changes
3. Nau, H. (1974). *National Politics and International Technology*. Baltimore, Johns Hopkins Press
   A very critical look at European attempts at cooperation in nuclear energy in the 1950s and 1960s
4. Pavitt, K. (1976). 'The Choice of Targets and Instruments for Government Support of Scientific Research.' In *The Economics of Industrial Subsidies*, Ed. A. Whiting. London, HMSO
   Describes and criticizes government policies towards industrial R & D. Argues that UK government expenditures on university research, and industry's expenditures on R & D, are low by international standards.

FURTHER

Technology in Western Europe
5. Layton, C. (1969). *European Advanced Technology: A Programme for Integration*. London, Allen and Unwin
   A strong advocate of closer European technological cooperation. The book also describes science and technology policies in the main European countries
6. Servan-Schreiber, J. (1968). *The American Challenge*. Santa Barbara, Hamilton
   Published in France in 1967. Important book that expressed growing apprehensions about American penetration and dominance of the Western European economy
7. Rowthorn, R. and Hymer, S. (1970). 'Multinational Corporations and International Oligopoly: the non-American Challenge.' In *The*

International Corporation. Ed. C. Kindleberger. Cambridge, Mass., MIT Press

Argues that fears of US takeover of Europe were misplaced and that the real problem is the growth of multinational corporations
8. OECD (1972). *The Research System: Volume 1,* France, West Germany, United Kingdom; *Volume 2:* Belgium, Netherlands, Sweden, Switzerland. Paris, OECD

A series of detailed studies on the organization of and role of fundamental research
9. Vernon, R. (Ed.) (1974). *Big Business and the State.* London, Macmillan

Excellent series of articles on industrial politics in the main Western European countries

United Kingdom
10. Central Advisory Council for Science and Technology (1968). *Technological Innovation in Britain.* London, HMSO

The Report of the Council attributes poor British innovation performance to ineffective use of manpower and weak marketing
11. Vig, N. (1968). *Science and Technology in British Politics.* Oxford, Pergamon Press

This should have been an important book, but is not because it is more concerned with the minutiae of politics than policy issues
12. Peck, M. (1968). 'Science and Technology.' In *Britain's Economy Prospects.* Ed. R. Caves. Washington, Brookings Institution

See Chapter 10. Excellent analysis, which recommends fewer funds for the aircraft industry
13. Clarke, R. (1973). 'Mintech in Perspective.' *Omega,* 1, Nos. 1 and 2

Frank account by a high civil servant of his experience at the Ministry of Technology
14. Gardner, N. (1976). 'Economics of Launching Aid.' In *The Economics of Industrial Subsidies.* Ed. A. Whiting. London, HMSO

Demonstrates, in simple financial terms, the extent of the failure in British Government support to the aircraft industry since 1945
15. Wonder, E. (1976). 'Decision making and reorganisation of the British nuclear power industry.' *Research Policy,* 5, No. 3, 240–269

Argues that the failure in British nuclear energy policy has its roots in insular nationalism, and the power of the nuclear lobby in the Atomic Energy Authority
16. Jones, D.T. (1976). 'Output, employment and labour productivity in Europe since 1955.' *National Institute Economic Review,* No. 77, August

A recent calculation of the extent of British industrial backwardness compared with continental Europe
17. Hobsbawm, E. (1969). *Industry and Empire.* London, Penguin

Evidence that UK technical and industrial backwardness is not new. Compare with Hamilton, A. (1976). 'The State of Industry after a Generation of Decline.' *Financial Times*, 26 July

France
18. OECD (1966). *Reviews of National Science Policy: France.* Paris, OECD
Now somewhat dated but still useful for background information
19. Gilpin, R. (1968). *France in the Age of the Scientific State.* Princeton, Princeton University Press
An excellent analysis of de Gaulle's policy towards science and technology
20. Saint-Geours, J. (1968). 'France's Scientific Policy.' In *Decision Making in National Science Policy*. Ed. A. de Reuck and M. Goldsmith. Report of Ciba Foundation Symposium. London, Churchill
A high official of the Ministry of Finance describes French institutions and official policy
21. Papon, P. (1973). 'Research Planning in French Science Policy: An Assessment.' *Research Policy*, **2**, *No. 3*
Detailed study of the working of national science planning in France. See also Ref. 1
22. Pavitt, K. (1977). 'Theory and Practice in Governmental Support for Industrial Research and Development.' *Minerva*, to be published
Describes and assesses the important changes in French policy since Valery Giscard d'Estaing became President
23. Carre, J.-J., Dubois, P. and Malinvaud, E. (1975). *French Economic Growth.* Oxford, Oxford University Press
A detailed account of French economic growth since World War II. Part 2 assesses the various causes

West Germany
24. Geimer, R. (1972). *Science in the Federal Republic of Germany.* 2nd edn. Godesberg, Bonn-bad
Detailed account, mainly for reference
25. Multelsee, W. (1970). 'German Federal Republic.' In *Technological Innovation and the Economy*, 43–50. Ed. M. Goldsmith. New York, Wiley-Interscience
An official West German view
26. (1976). *Fifth Report of the Federal Government on Research.* Bonn, Federal Ministry for Research and Technology
Good statistics and statements of official Government policy. See also Ref. 4

Other West European countries
27. Dorfer, I. (1974). 'Science and Technology in Sweden: The Fabians versus Europe.' *Research Policy*, **3**, No. 2, 134–155

A lively account of development in Swedish technology policy. Argues that a basic conflict exists between domestic pressures towards equality and government intervention, and the requirements of international competitiveness

28. OECD (1975). *Patterns of Resources devoted to Research and Experimental Development in the OECD Area, 1963–1971,* and *Changing Priorities for Government R & D.* Paris, OECD
Comprehensive and comparable statistical data on R & D trends in the main OECD countries
29. EEC (1974). *Expenditure on Research and Development in the Community Countries: Analysis by Objectives. 1969–1973.* Brussells, EEC
Detailed comparison of R & D expenditures by the Governments of the Common Market Countries. See also Refs. 8 and 9

European cooperation
30. Bondi, H. (1973). 'International Collaboration in Advanced Technology.' *The World Today,* **29**, No. 1, 16–23
Observations about European collaboration, based on experience as Head of the European Space Research Organisation
31. Pavitt, K. (1972). 'Technology in Europe's Future.' *Research Policy,* **1**, No. 3
Argues that much closer political consensus is a necessary prerequisite for effective European technological cooperation
32. Williams, R. (1973). *European Technology: The Politics of Collaboration.* London, Croom Helm
Another sceptical look at European cooperation. See also Ref. 4

Questions

What have been the major objectives of European science and technology since the Second World War? What problems have been encountered meeting these objectives? Distinguish any important changes over time and differences between countries. (See Refs. 1–4.)

What has been the outcome of the French political objectives of 'technological independence and national power'? (See Refs. 1, 3, 18–23.)

What has been the role of science and technology in West Germany's attempts to find an international political position commensurate with its economic position? (See Refs. 2, 3, 24–26.)

Points for discussion or essays

It is often argued that, since the UK has consistently spent more on R & D than any other country in Western Europe, and has had a consistently worse economic performance, then R & D has little to do with British industrial regeneration. Do you agree? If not, why not? (See Refs. 4, 8, 10, 12, 14, 28.)

'The states of Europe need each other to pursue effective research and development. They also need to develop common features in the national organisation of science and technology if they are to work together' (C. Layton (1969)). Comment on the implications of this statement and its relevance to European R & D policy in the 1970s. (See Refs. 3, 5, 30–32.)

'Scientific knowledge is, and always has been, international. In recent years, however, scientific research as such has also become increasingly international and this is due to complexity and expense' (Sir Brian Flowers, former Chairman of the Science Research Council). Comment on this view in the light of the experience of Western Europe. (See Refs. 3, 5, 30–32.)

Compare and contrast the experience of Britain, France and West Germany in policies for science and technology since the Second World War. What lessons do you think can be drawn from these activities? Comment on how you think future policy is likely to develop. (See Refs. 1, 2, 4, 5, 8–26.)

Appendix: Statistics on Science and Technology

With increasing amounts of resources and more people involved in science and technology, the pressures to collect more complete statistical information on scientific and technological activities have grown. These statistics cannot in themselves tell us how much resources we should devote to science and technology as a whole, or to specific scientific or technological fields. Nor can they tell us what the purposes of science and technology should be, but they can give us a better basis for understanding what the present situation is, and for debating how it could or should change in the future. The purpose of this note is to give a brief, introductory description of the current state of statistics on science and technology.

Table 1 shows total expenditures on R & D as a percentage of Gross National Product in a number of OECD countries. Data for such expenditures prior to the 1960s are much more sparse, but they show a steady increase in the percentage of national resources devoted to R & D until the mid-1960s when, as *Table 1* shows, the percentage stabilized in some countries and even began to decrease.

Table 2 shows, for the same countries, who paid for the R & D and who performed it in 1969. For example, reading across the page: for R & D in France, business provides 33% of the money, government 62% and higher education 1%; 56% of the work is done by business, 29% by government and 14% by higher education. In all these countries, government and business (privately and publicly owned) provide the lion's share of the funds, industry performs more than half of all R & D (except for Canada), and the universities depend heavily on government money. However, as *Table 3* shows, the degree to which industry also depends on government money varies considerably between countries, and there were some noticeable shifts in this degree of dependence during the 1960s.

In addition, *Table 4* (columns II) show that the degree of dependance on government money varies considerably between industry as well as between countries. The same *Table 4* (columns I) show that, in spite of significant differences amongst the countries in the pattern of R & D in industry, the same groups of industrial sectors (electrical, chemical, aircraft, and instruments and machinery) account for more than half and often for more than 70% of all the R & D performed in industry.

Governments finance R & D for a variety of purposes, and *Table 5* shows in what proportions the funds went to various policy objectives during the 1960s. In many countries, military, space and nuclear R & D accounted for a very large proportion, although in six of the seven countries listed, this category became relatively less important during the 1960s. Since 1973, however, government expenditures on nuclear energy R & D have increased considerably.

The comparison of R & D expenditures between different countries, and between different periods of time, presents difficulties because the costs of R & D inputs can and do vary between countries and over time. For example, in the first international comparison of R & D expenditures in W. Europe, the USA and the USSR in 1962, Freeman and Young calculated that European research input costs were about 60% of those in the USA.

Table 6 compares industrial R & D expenditures in 1963 US dollars in a number of countries in 1963 and 1973; in the absence of an index of R & D prices, the price index for Gross Product is used in order to correct for increasing R & D costs between 1963 and 1973. Given the conclusions of Freeman and Young, the figures in this table underestimate the magnitude of R & D effort in Western European countries and Japan, when compared with those of the USA. It is clear, however, that industry-financed R & D activities increased considerably between 1963 and 1973 in all countries except the UK.

Another method of comparing R & D in different countries and over time is to measure R & D manpower as well as R & D expenditure. However, this also raises difficulties because the available manpower statistics are not so plentiful, because manpower comparisons do not take account of differences in quality of equipment and support services, and because someone called a technician in one country is called a qualified research worker in another. This last difficulty can be reduced by grouping together scientists, engineers and technicians in any international comparison.

Only between 20 and 30% of qualified scientists and engineers in the OECD countries are employed in R & D activities, so it is also important to know about the deployment of all scientists and engineers, in R & D and elsewhere. In 1971, in the UK, 62% of them were employed in industry (42% of scientists, 77% of engineers)[3]. The pattern of employment of all scientists and engineers in British industry is similar to that for R & D expenditures (as shown in *Table 4*), except that the relative weights of the aircraft and the machinery industries are reversed.

Measuring the output of research and development

R & D statistics measure *inputs* of financial resources and manpower. They do not measure the resulting *outputs* of information and innovations. C. Freeman has set out in systematic detail the possibilities and problems of using scientific papers, patents and other things as measures of R & D outputs[4]. In spite of the considerable problems involved, significant progress has been made in the past few years in measuring R & D outputs. The publications by the US National Science Foundation, entitled *Science Indicators*[5], are becoming an invaluable source of statistics attempting to measure R & D outputs.

In addition, the US Department of Commerce is now publishing regular reports on trends in patenting in the USA[6]. For example, *Figure 1* shows trends in the percentage of US patents taken out by

Figure 1 Annual foreign share of US patents of selected countries (Source: *Technology Assessment and Forecast.* Initial Publication (1973a), Early Warning Report (1973b), Third Report (1974), Fourth Report (1975a), Fifth Report (1975b). Washington, US Department of Commerce)

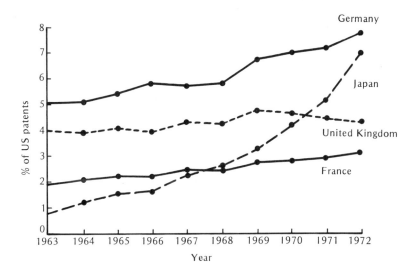

foreign countries between 1963 and 1972. It shows the rapid growth of Japan, the considerable increase of W. Germany, the slow increase from a low level of France, and the stagnation of the UK. These trends are entirely consistent with those shown in *Table 6.* In addition, however, *Figure 1* shows that, already in 1963, W. German industry was probably undertaking a significantly greater innovative effort than UK industry.

References

1. OECD (1970). *The Measurement of Scientific and Technical Activities.* Paris, OECD

2. Freeman, C. and Young, A. (1965). *The Research and Development Effort.* Paris, OECD
3. (1970). *Statistics of Science and Technology: 1970.* London, HMSO
4. Freeman, C. (1974). *The Economics of Industrial Innovation*, 332–387. London, Penguin
5. National Science Board (1975). *Science Indicators, 1974.* Washington, National Science Foundation
6. See the reports published by the Office of Technology Assessment and Forecast, US Department of Commerce, Washington

Table 1   Trends in total expenditures on R & D as a percentage of Gross National Product

Country	1963/4	1967	1969	1971
Belgium	0.9	1.1	1.1	1.2
France	1.7	2.2	1.9	1.8
West Germany	1.4	1.7	1.7	2.1
Italy	0.6	0.7	0.8	0.9
Netherlands	1.9	2.1	2.0	2.0
UK	2.3	2.4	2.3	2.3
USA	2.7	3.1	2.8	2.5
Canada	1.0	1.3	1.3	1.2
Japan	1.3	1.3	1.5	1.6
Sweden	1.3	1.4	1.3	1.6

Source: OECD (1975). *Patterns of Resources Devoted To Research and Experimental Development in the OECD Areas, 1963–71.* Paris, OECD

Table 2   Main sources of funds and sectors of performance for R & D in 1969 (percentage of total expenditure in each country)

Country	Business		Government		Higher education	
	S	P	S	P	S	P
France	33	56	62	29	1	14
West Germany	60	68	39	5	0	18
Italy	50	55	41	25	7	20
Netherlands	59	62	38	11	0	18
UK	44	65	51	25	1	8
USA	38	70	58	14	3	13
Canada	30	37	54	35	13	29
Japan	68	67	14	12	18	19
Sweden	57	66	40	15	4	19

Source: *Science Policy*, Sept/Oct, 1972. S = Source of funds for R & D; P = Performance of R & D

Table 3 Government-financed R & D as a percentage of all R & D performed in industry

Country	1953	1957	1961	1963	1964	1965	1967	1969	1971	Industry financed R & D as a percentage of GNP (1971)
Belgium	—	—	—	5.0	—	—	7.0	—	—	0.6
France	—	—	33.0	30.0	—	37.0	39.0	39.0	—	0.6
West Germany	—	—	—	—	14.0	—	17.0	13.0	—	1.1
Italy	—	—	—	1.0	—	3.0	2.0	3.0	—	0.5
Netherlands	—	—	—	—	1.0	—	1.0	4.0	—	1.1
UK	—	—	41.0	—	36.0	—	32.0	—	—	1.0
USA	39.0	56.0	56.0	57.0	—	54.0	49.0	46.0	41.0	1.0
Canada	—	—	—	13.0	—	17.0	14.0	15.0	—	0.4
Japan	—	—	—	0	—	—	1.0	1.0	—	1.2
Sweden	—	—	—	—	27.0	—	22.0	14.0	—	0.9

Sources: OECD (1971). *R & D in OECD Member Countries: Trends and Objectives,* Table 9. Paris, OECD. *Patterns of R & D Resources; 1953—71,* NSF 70—46. Washington, National Science Foundation. Same as Table 1

Table 4   Distribution of R & D performance by industry and the importance of government-financed R & D in each industry (1969) (% age)

Sector	France I	France II	W. Germany I	W. Germany II	Italy I	Italy II	UK I	UK II	USA I	USA II	Canada I	Canada II	Japan I	Japan II	Sweden I	Sweden II
Electrical & electronic	25	34	28	10	23	11	23	33	23	54	27	19	27	19	24	11
Chemicals, drugs, petroleum	17	5	29	1	25	0	14	3	13	10	19	3	23	0	11	1
Aircraft	23	87	7	99	0	n.a.	25	84	31	78	13	42	0	0	14	51
Motor vehicles, ships, other transport	9	38	15	1	25	0	–	6	9	2	2	18	11	0	–	12
Metals and metal products	3	6	5	2	4	5	4	4	2	5	9	5	8	0	14	12
Instruments and machinery	8	28	9	18	4	1	11	17	13	25	8	14	11	2	18	1
Food, drink, tobacco; textiles, leather, rubber, plastic products	4	4	2	7	8	1	6	2	3	n.a.	5	7	6	1	4	7
Stone, clay, glass; paper & printing, wood, furniture, other	2	6	2	9	1	2	4	3	2	n.a.	8	6	6	1	8	7
TOTAL MANUFACTURING	91	39	96	13	89	3	94	34	96	46	91	15	92	1	92	13
Services (construction, transport communications, other)	8	5	3	33	11	41	5	2	4	69	6	5	7	7	5	23
Mining	n.a.	n.a.	1	22	0	0	1	0	n.a.	n.a.	3	7	1	2	1	3
TOTAL BUSINESS ENTERPRIZE	100	36	100	13	100	7	100	32	100	47	100	15	100	1	100	14

I = percentage of total business enterprize R & D performed in the sector; II = percentage of total R & D in each sector that is financed by government

Source: OECD (1972). *International Survey of the Resources Devoted to R & D in 1969 by OECD Member-Countries*, Vol. 1, *Business Enterprise Sector*. Paris, OECD

Table 5 Percentage shares of public R & D expenditures

Country	1960—1961				1970—1971			
	Military, space, nuclear	Economic, agric. manufacturing services	Welfare, health, environment	Other, incl. university	Military, space, nuclear	Economic, agric. manufacturing services	Welfare, health, environment	Other, incl. university
USA	89	3	7	1	78	7	11	4
Canada	44	32	3	20	29	50	12	9
UK	80	11	2	8	49	22	1	28
Japan*	13	33	3	51	10	23	4	63
Sweden*	73	7	5	15	42	17	11	28
Netherlands	17	24	10	50	17	17	12	52
France	69	8	1	22	51	18	2	29
West Germany	n.a.	n.a.	n.a.	n.a.	35	9	7	49

*Data for 1969—1970 and not 1970—1971.
Source: Freeman, C. *et al.* (1971). 'The Goals of R & D in the 1970's'. *Science Studies*, Vol. 1, 357—406, for 1960—1961; same as Table 1 for 1970—1971.

Table 6 Expenditures on industrial R & D in the major OECD countries, 1963 and 1973 (US $ million, 1963, GDP deflation used)

Year	1963				1973			
Source of funds	Industry and government		Industry only		Industry and government		Industry only	
Unit / Country	US $ millions (1963)	US = 100	US $ millions (1963)	US = 100	US $ millions (1963)	US = 100	US $ millions (1963)	US = 100
USA	12 630	100	5360	100	14 379	100	8 728	100
France	966 (1966)	7.6 (1966)	552 (1966)	10.3 (1966)	1 390	9.7	930	10.7
West Germany	843 (1964)	6.7 (1964)	776 (1964)	14.5 (1964)	1 897	13.2	1 525	17.5
Italy	180	1.4	179	3.3	406 (1972)	2.8 (1972)	384 (1972)	4.4 (1972)
Netherlands	167 (1964)	1.3 (1964)	165 (1964)	3.1 (1964)	255	1.8	242	2.8
UK	1286 (1964)	10.2 (1964)	838 (1964)	15.6 (1964)	1 333	9.3	855	9.8
Sweden	156	1.2	113	2.1	275	1.9	223	2.6
Western European Countries	3598	28.4	2623	48.9	5 557	38.7	4 159	47.8
Western European Countries less UK	2312	18.2	1785	33.3	4 224	29.4	3 304	38.0
Japan	575	4.6	573	10.7	2 107	14.7	2 004	23.6
TOTAL (US $ millions 1963)	16 803		8556		22 043		14 951	

Source: OECD (1974). *Trends in Industrial Research and Development.* Document SSTI/SPR/75. Paris, OECD